DID JOSEPH SMITH HAVE TO TAKE ALGEBRA?

Did Joseph Smith Have to Take Algebra?

Shane Barker

CFI
An Imprint of Cedar Fort, Inc.
Springville, Utah

ISBN 13: 978-1-4621-1117-6

Published by CFI, an imprint of Cedar Fort, Inc.
2373 W. 700 S., Springville, UT 84663
Distributed by Cedar Fort, Inc. www.cedarfort.com

LIBRARY OF CONGRESS CATALOGING-IN-PUBLICATION DATA

Barker, Shane R., author.
Did Joseph Smith have to take algebra? : following the example of Joseph Smith / Shane Barker.
pages cm
ISBN 978-1-4621-1117-6 (alk. paper)
1. Christian life--Mormon authors. 2. Smith, Joseph, 1805-1844. I. Title.

BX8656.B365 2012
248.4'89332--dc23

2012032787

Cover design by Erica Dixon
Cover design © 2012 by Lyle Mortimer
Edited and typeset by Casey J. Winters

Printed in the United States of America

10 9 8 7 6 5 4 3 2 1

FOR TANNER AND WADE

OTHER BOOKS BY SHANE BARKER

Stepping Up, Taking Charge and Leading the Way:
A Guide for Teenage Leaders

I Thought Scout Uniforms Were Fireproof:
Putting the Fun in Scouting

Can't Hang Out . . . Gotta Build a Ship:
Unleashing Your Inner Nephi

TABLE OF CONTENTS

ONE

RUNAWAY STAGECOACH

FOLLOWING THE EXAMPLE OF JOSEPH SMITH

"John, hold on! I'll try and get to the horses!"

"Joseph, no!"

Dr. John Bernhisel grabbed hold of a slatted seat as the speeding stagecoach bounced over a rut. "You'll be killed!"

"We'll be killed if I don't!" Joseph Smith called back. "Now hold on!"

Joseph crouched in the door as the stagecoach careened over the bumpy road. A few minutes earlier, the coach had stopped at a country inn. Something spooked the horses after the driver stepped down, and they'd bolted. Now the animals were thundering down the road out of control, dragging the swaying, teetering stagecoach behind them.

Joseph grabbed frantically at the doorframe as the coach lurched, nearly pitching him out. He glanced over his shoulder, and his eyes widened in horror: a terrified woman was staggering toward the opposite door with her baby. To save its life, the woman was about to throw the child from the coach.

"No!" he shouted. "Madam, don't!"

"But she'll be killed!" the distraught mother wailed.

"Madam . . ."

Joseph turned to Dr. Bernhisel. "John, quickly!" he shouted. "Don't let her throw that child from the coach!"

"Please, madam," the doctor pleaded, lurching across the bouncing coach toward her. "Your daughter will be fine. There, now . . . please, just hold her tightly and she'll be fine."

Joseph turned back to the door. A moment earlier another passenger, a United States congressman, had thought of saving his own life by leaping from the coach. The man had stopped only after seeing how fast the stagecoach was thundering over the road.

"There, there," Dr. Bernhisel said, pulling the hysterical mother back to her seat. "Everything will be fine . . . just hold on now."

Joseph took a deep breath and then climbed through the narrow door and pulled himself onto the roof, the coach bouncing and swaying beneath him. Trunks, boxes, and other luggage had been piled high over the carriage, and the prophet had to clamber over the bulky bags to reach the coachman's seat. The horses were running flat out in front of him, their nostrils flaring fiercely in the hot air as their hooves pounded the road.

The coach dropped into a rut, tipping onto two wheels. Joseph grabbed frantically for a handrail, holding tightly until the coach righted itself, and then he reached for the reins. He pulled gently but firmly.

"Whoa, whoa there," he called out. "Whoa, now . . . whoa, whoa . . ."

The chuffing horses responded, tossing their heads and beginning to slow. Joseph pulled more firmly on the reins. He then reached down and eased back on the brake handle.

"Whoa, whoa there . . ."

The horses gradually slowed and—under Joseph's hand—finally came to a stop.

Joseph released his breath, letting his head drop to his chest. He closed his eyes and whispered a quick prayer of gratitude. He tied off the reins and swung down from the coach, opening the door and helping the shaken passengers to the ground.

"Thank you, young man," the rattled congressman said. He took Joseph's hand and shook it firmly. "Thank you! I, ah . . . I have never before seen an act of such bravery!"

"Nor have I," a second congressman said as he clambered gingerly to the ground. "When I return to Congress, I shall make mention of this incredible act of courage."

"You deserve our utmost gratitude," the first congressman declared. "Not to mention a substantial reward . . . which I shall see to the moment I return to Washington."

The Prophet Joseph was an outstanding role model. He set a powerful example that we can follow today.

Neither of the congressmen ever followed through with their promises, but that's beside the point. I love that story! It's not only a rattling good adventure (it sounds like something from an Indiana Jones movie, doesn't it?), but it shows a side of the Prophet Joseph Smith that's not generally known. And it reinforces my testimony that—on top of everything else—Joseph Smith was a remarkable man.

When you think of Joseph Smith, you might think of his First Vision. Or of his experiences with the angel Moroni and the gold plates. You might think of his visits with John the Baptist, the apostles Peter, James, and John, or other heavenly messengers. You might even think of his final, tragic sacrifice in Carthage Jail.

Joseph Smith stood fast when times were hard. He was loyal to his friends. He worked hard and did his best to learn. He demonstrated incredible courage. Over and over again he provided powerful, lasting examples of repentance, forgiveness, and sacrifice.

You can do the same!

But there was more to Joseph Smith than that. He did more than teach, preach, and inspire. In his short life he organized the Church of Jesus Christ of Latter-day Saints.

He translated the Book of Mormon. He founded the city of Nauvoo. He received volumes of revelations. He organized the Relief Society, which today is the largest women's organization in the world. He was so loved and so friendly, so warm, honest, and approachable, that his people referred to him as "Brother Joseph."

On top of all that, the Prophet Joseph was an outstanding role model. As a young boy—and later as a teenager—he demonstrated incredible courage. He stood fast in times of trials and discouragement. He worked hard and, with limited schooling, did his best to learn. He was faithful and loyal to his family and friends . . . even when some betrayed or deserted him. Over and over again he provided powerful, lasting examples of repentance, forgiveness, and sacrifice.

He set a wonderful example.

> What's your favorite story about the Prophet Joseph? Is there anything you can learn from that story? Something you can apply right now to things happening in your life? What is it?

"Nephi taught us to liken the scriptures to ourselves," my tenth-grade seminary teacher once told us. "And we can liken Joseph Smith's experiences to our lives too. The Prophet's example can be an inspiration when we're facing tough times or when we're dealing with tough challenges. When Joseph Smith had problems or questions, for instance, what did *he* do?"

"He prayed!" someone shouted.

"That's right. Just think about the first time he walked into a grove of trees to ask his Heavenly Father a question . . . Can you imagine how different your life would be if Joseph Smith hadn't had the courage to pray?"

Brother Sanders's voice softened as he talked, and we all knew why. He'd once told us of a profound experience he'd had in answer to prayer; the story had left the entire class teary eyed.

> Elder Joseph B. Wirthlin once said: "The more I know of the Prophet Joseph, the more I love him, the more I yearn to follow his example, the more I appreciate what our Father in Heaven and His Son have done in restoring this gospel that is destined to fill the earth in these, the latter days" ("You'll Grow into It," *New Era*, Nov. 2000, 4).

He looked around for a moment, finally focusing his attention upon my friend Ethan.

"Ethan, what about you? Do you think Joseph Smith's example could help you to deal with challenges in *your* life?"

"I don't think so," Ethan said sadly.

"Oh? And why not?"

"Because I'm failing algebra."

The class howled (as Ethan turned the color of a ripe grape). Then just as everyone was settling down again, a young woman named Emily said, "Actually, Ethan, Joseph Smith would have *loved* algebra."

Ethan wrinkled his nose skeptically. "Really?"

"Sure! After all, math is the one class Heavenly Father expects you to be really good at."

Ethan blinked. "You're kidding . . . *math*?"

"Sure!" Emily said. "Remember? He said to 'go forth and multiply'!"

The class howled again. (Brother Sanders shook his head, realizing it was going to be one of *those* days.)

Is there one aspect of the Prophet Joseph's character that you especially admire? His loyalty, for instance? Or his courage, his faith, his warmth, or his friendliness?

What's one thing you could do today to develop that quality in *your* life?

But Ethan suddenly brightened. "Hey," he said, sitting up straight in his seat. "That's it!"

"That's what?"

"The answer . . . It's reformed Egyptian!"

"*What*?"

"Joseph had to translate reformed Egyptian, right?"

"Yes . . ."

"Well, I bet that stuff looked just like my algebra!"

Ethan beamed proudly. "If Joseph Smith could understand it, then so can I!"

The class howled again (I think Brother Sanders was beginning to regret not becoming a dentist or something). Our teacher finally got the class back on track again, but I wasn't really paying attention anymore.

I was still thinking about fourteen-year-old Joseph walking into the woods to pray.

And I was thinking about Brother Sanders's question: "Can you imagine how different your life would be if Joseph Smith hadn't had the courage to pray?"

We live in a time of unique challenges, dangers, and temptations. And more than ever, we need the power of good examples to guide us. We need worthy role models and heroes whom we can look up to, follow, and emulate.

We need heroes like Joseph Smith.

The truth is that a certain problem had been troubling me. And when Brother Sanders mentioned prayer, I realized that he'd given me the answer I was looking for.

When I later followed Joseph Smith's example and prayed, the answer I received wasn't as dramatic as his . . . but it was just as real. I learned that day that the Prophet Joseph's experiences *could* apply to my life. Prayer worked for Joseph Smith. It worked for Brother Sanders. It worked for me, and it will work for you.

But Joseph Smith's example didn't stop there. You know, for instance, that the Prophet had great faith.

And *you* can have great faith too.

You know that Joseph Smith was blessed and guided by promptings of the Holy Ghost.

You too can receive promptings of the Spirit, allowing it to guide, bless, and protect you.

You know that Joseph was courageous in the face of adversity.

And you can be courageous too. When times are tough, you can follow the Prophet Joseph's example and stand fast. You can learn to be a little stronger and to hold on a little longer. In fact, you can develop any of the traits that not only made Joseph Smith a great prophet but that set him apart as an extraordinary person.

And that's what this book is about. It's about taking the example of the Prophet Joseph Smith and applying it to *your* life. It's about learning the lessons that Joseph taught—by example—and using them to tackle the challenges you face every day.

> When times are tough, you can follow the Prophet Joseph's example and stand fast. You can be a little stronger and hold on a little longer.

PARABLE OF THE HOPPERS

I once heard a story about baby locusts (often called "hoppers"). Because of their thick, stubby bodies, they can't fly without a lot of help. They can *soar* on wind currents if they become airborne, but they can't take off by themselves.

So they spend their time hopping around on the ground. And when a breeze comes up they jump . . . and if they jump high enough, the wind picks them up and carries them around like miniature gliders. Researchers say hoppers can reach altitudes of almost two miles and that they can soar as far as eighty miles in a single day!

So picture the little hopper. As he's hopping around with his nose in the dirt, the breeze picks up.

The wind begins rustling the leaves in the trees.

And the little hopper hears the leaves rustling and realizes, *Now's my chance . . . It's my turn to soar*!

So the little hopper takes a deep breath, gets ready, and then jumps as high as he can. And the next thing he knows, he's soaring high above the earth.

Now, I think many of our heroes in the scriptures had similar experiences. When David saw the giant Goliath terrorizing the Israelite army—when even the strongest, fiercest warriors were cowering in fear at the sight of the giant—David heard the leaves rustling and thought, *This is my chance. It's my turn to do something special*!

When Nephi looked out over the ocean and thought about the challenge of building a ship, he heard the leaves rustling and thought, *With the Lord's help I can do this. It's my turn to do something extraordinary*!

When a mighty Lamanite army invaded the land, Helaman's two thousand young, inexperienced warriors heard the leaves rustling and thought, *This is our chance. It's our turn to make a difference*!

When enemies scattered King Lamoni's sheep and the other servants ran for their lives, Ammon heard the rustling in the leaves and—standing there all alone and outnumbered—thought, *I can do this. This is my chance to work a miracle*!

And when Joseph Smith had his incredible visions—when he listened to the Lord and then later to Moroni and other heavenly messengers and pictured the awesome mission he had ahead of him—he heard the rustling in the leaves and thought, *It's my turn now . . . and I'm going to make a difference*!

Remember that Joseph Smith didn't have it all that easy. The powers of darkness attacked the young prophet before he even finished his first prayer.

He was persecuted and ridiculed from the moment he began sharing his fantastic story.

Do you think that was easy?

I don't!

And I think it would have been easy for him to give up. But he'd heard the rustling in the leaves. He realized it was *his* turn. And he accepted the challenge.

Now what about you? The Lord held you in reserve for thousands of years. He waited until the forces of evil were stronger than ever, when he needed the strongest, most valiant, trustworthy servants he had before sending you here.

And now he needs you to do something special with your life. Can you hear the leaves rustling?

It's *your* turn!

President Thomas S. Monson once said, "All of us living in the world today need points of reference—even models to follow. . . .

". . . [And] no description of models for us to follow would be complete without including Joseph Smith, the first prophet of this dispensation" ("Models to Follow," *Ensign*, Nov. 2002, 60).

So how do you follow the example of the Prophet Joseph?

I'm glad you asked!

The following discovery will give you a couple of good, solid ideas!

FOOTSTEPS OF THE PROPHET

If you could boil all of the problems, challenges, questions, and worries you face every day into one single dilemma, what would it be?

Now suppose you were able to ask the Prophet Joseph for suggestions in dealing with that. What do you think he might say?

What's one thing you could do right now to put that counsel into action? (Why not go do it!)

Do you think Joseph Smith would have been patient in your situation? Would he have been resourceful? Prayerful? Courageous? Cheerful? Would he have become discouraged and given up, or would he have worked until he solved the problem?

What's one thing you could do right now to demonstrate that attitude? (And go do it!)

Are you currently reading the Book of Mormon? If not, start today! Set a goal to read a page or a chapter every day. Enjoy the blessings that come from daily scripture study!

What do you think Joseph's attitude would be as he dealt with your problem? Would he have complained? Grumbled? Whined? Wondered why everything bad always happened to him? Or would he have trusted his Heavenly Father to see that everything worked out for him? **(And what should your attitude be?)**

What's something you could do today—right now—that Joseph Smith might have done to solve the problem or make it easier to deal with? (*Go do it!*)

All done?

Great!

I love doing these "discoveries." They help me to channel my thoughts and feelings in good, positive directions. I hope you'll take advantage of the ones I've included in this book.

Let me give you one more thought before we wrap up:

THIS MIGHT BE THE DAY

Several years ago I joined the National Ski Patrol and began patrolling at a nearby resort. Once, during our morning meeting, a patroller stood up and said, "This might be the day you save a life. It might be the day you make a difference."

That thought hit me like a thunderbolt. And I went out thinking, this might be the day I save a life!

It might be the day I help someone who really needs it.

It might be the day I bless a life.

It might be the day I make a difference!

Wow! What a difference that made to me! I went out every day looking for ways to help and for ways to serve.

And the exciting thing is, you can do the same thing!

Think about this: today might be the day that

- you make a difference to someone.
- you become friends with someone who really needs one.
- you cheer someone up.
- you give new hope to someone.
- you set the right example for someone who needs it.
- you encourage someone who's feeling down.
- you make someone feel important.
- you make someone feel loved.
- you change a life!

Now, let's back up a little bit. Remember Joseph Smith on the stagecoach? When he climbed into that coach, he didn't know he'd be needed to do anything important that day. But when the chips were down and the Lord needed a hero, he didn't hesitate.

He stepped up.

And he made a difference.

You can do the same thing!

So that's it! This was a fun book to write. And I hope you'll have fun reading it.

Let's get started!

TWO

ANGELS, MOOSE, AND FAMILY HOME EVENING

STRENGTHENING YOUR FAMILY

For the third time in an hour, seventeen-year-old Joseph Smith stumbled in the soft dirt of the wheat field. He caught himself before he fell but had to drop his scythe for a moment to rub his eyes.

A short distance away, his older brother Alvin was slicing a freshly sharpened scythe smoothly through the golden wheat.

He makes it look so easy, Joseph thought as he watched.

Rather than simply swinging the tool—or hacking away with it (as Joseph did when he was tired)—Alvin had a way of slicing the blade easily through the wheat as he worked, cutting the stalks cleanly.

William and Don Carlos—Joseph's youngest brothers—were following Alvin dutifully, gathering the freshly cut wheat and tying it into sheaves. Joseph yawned as he watched them and then reached up to rub his eyes again. He was so tired that he was practically asleep on his feet.

A short time earlier, Alvin had chided him for his sluggishness.

"C'mon, Joseph," he'd said with a note of reproach. "We have to finish this field before noon." He'd glanced across the field to where their father was cutting a neat swath through the wheat.

"We can't be slacking off when Father's depending on us."

"I'm sorry," Joseph had said. "I'll do better."

Alvin punched his younger brother playfully before going back to work. "I know you will."

Joseph yawned. The truth was that he was working as hard as he could. But he was exhausted. And his mind was miles and miles from the wheat field.

It had been three years since his remarkable vision in the Sacred Grove. He'd begun to wonder where he stood in the eyes of the Lord, and—before going to bed the night before—he had knelt in prayer. And he'd received a marvelous visit from an angel named Moroni.

Moroni appeared to Joseph three times that night, telling him of sacred records buried in a nearby hill and announcing that God had important work for him. The visits lasted the entire night—after a full day of working in the fields—which was why Joseph was so tired now.

But there was something else troubling him. Before concluding his night-long visits, Moroni told Joseph to tell his father everything he had seen and heard that night.

But Joseph hadn't done so.

Suddenly, a hand was on Joseph's shoulder, startling him into wakefulness. He looked up to see his father, realizing that he'd been sleeping on his feet.

"What's wrong?" Joseph Smith Sr. asked, looking his son up and down as if searching for some sort of injury. "Are you sick?"

"No, Father," Joseph said. "I'm sorry . . . I'll get back to work."

"Joseph." The man took his son by the shoulders and looked into his eyes. "Go home," he said. "You need to rest."

"No," Joseph replied. "I'll be fine. I just needed to catch my breath—"

"Joseph," his father repeated, a little more firmly this time. "Go home. Get some rest. If you feel better, you can join us again this afternoon."

Ashamed at having let his father down, Joseph started for home. But he was dead tired. As he was crossing a fence, he slipped and fell.

And for a while darkness was all he knew.

"Joseph."

Joseph heard a voice calling his name.

"Joseph."

The voice was deep and familiar. It was as soft as a whisper but had such power that it penetrated to his very core.

"Joseph."

He slowly opened his eyes. He was lying on his back in the field where he'd fallen. And standing above him in a brilliant pillar of light was Moroni, the angel who'd spent the night instructing him.

I don't know if Joseph was surprised to see Moroni again. But the angel's words cut him to the quick.

"Why did you not tell your father that which I commanded you to tell him?"

Joseph was stunned. I can't imagine what it was like being chastised by an angel. But he answered truthfully.

"I was afraid that he wouldn't believe me."

Moroni instructed Joseph to return to his father in the field, and to tell him everything he had seen and learned. And—as if to relieve Joseph's anxiety—the angel promised that his father would "believe every word you say to him" (Lucy Mack Smith, *Revised and Enhanced History of Joseph Smith by His Mother* [Salt Lake City: Deseret Book, 1997] 79).

> How would *you* like to confess to an angel that you hadn't done what he'd asked?
>
> How would you like to confess that to *Moroni*? (Be kinda scary, huh?)
>
> Can you imagine what that was like for Joseph Smith?

I'd like to stop the story here for a moment. You see, I've often wondered why it was so important that Joseph tell his father about Moroni's visit. I mean, what was the big deal? Was it to ask for help understanding the angel's message?

No.

To ask for time off to search for the plates?

No.

To ask for a ride to the Hill Cumorah?

Still no.

I think it was simply because Joseph Smith Sr. was Joseph's *father*. And Moroni knew that parents ought to know about important events in their children's lives.

Now there's an important lesson there. Did you catch it? More important, do *you* share important thoughts, concerns, and events with *your* parents?

The Prophet Joseph knew that his parents were valuable sources of advice and wisdom. Several years after his first experience with Moroni, the Prophet's father became ill, and Joseph prayed fervently for his recovery. He said that he wanted to once more "be blessed with

> President Thomas S. Monson has said, "Talk to your mother and to your father. It may be difficult to realize, but your parents have lived through many of the same challenges which you face today. Often they see the big picture more clearly than you can. They pray for you each day and are entitled to the inspiration of our Heavenly Father in providing you counsel and advice" ("Constant Truths for Changing Times," *Ensign*, May 2005, 19).

his company and advice, esteeming it one of the greatest earthly blessings to be blessed with the society of parents, whose mature years and experience render them capable of administering the most wholesome advice" (*History of the Church*, 4:604).

I know exactly what Joseph meant. The night before I left for my mission to Japan, I was suddenly overcome by a flood of doubts. I was excited to serve my Heavenly Father, but I was also scared. And worried. I wondered if I was ready to be a missionary and whether I'd be a good missionary.

I wondered if I *could* be a good missionary.

I knew that I should go straight to my parents to talk about it. But on top of everything else, I didn't want to seem weak or uncommitted.

And I didn't want to admit that I was scared.

Fortunately, my father knew that something was wrong. And he came to talk to me, calming me down and reassuring me. He knew exactly what I needed to hear that night, and he knew exactly what he needed to say. To this day I'm grateful for that simple talk . . . the last one we had for two years.

You need to know that your parents are there for you too. So don't be afraid to share your life with them. Share your thoughts, your dreams, and your triumphs . . . and let them support and encourage you when you're troubled, worried, or confused.

After all, that's what they're there for.

Let them help!

BE TRUTHFUL

There's another part of Joseph's experience with Moroni that's always impressed me. When Joseph told his father about his heavenly visitor, Joseph Smith Sr. believed him.

Every word.

Now, there might be many reasons for that. But I think it's partly because Father Smith *knew* that his son was a truthful boy. He knew from experience that Joseph didn't lie, so he had no reason to doubt his fantastic story. He told Joseph that it was "of God" and counseled him to do exactly as Moroni commanded him.

> Think of a time you really needed the trust of *your* parents. On a scale of 1 to 5, how much did you *deserve* that trust?
>
> **1 2 3 4 5**
>
> Is there anything you could have done to be even more deserving of that trust?
>
> And what about now? If you suddenly needed your parents to completely, absolutely trust you, would they?
>
> How much do you deserve their trust?
>
> **1 2 3 4 5**
>
> If you circled anything but 5, what could you do today to improve?

While you're a teenager, there will be times when you'll need the trust of *your* parents too. You might need to explain a poor grade on your report card or a fresh dent in the family car. When those times come, will your parents—like Joseph's—know you to be a truthful teenager too?

I hope so!

And if your track record needs improving, it's not too late. Begin today! No matter what else is happening, be sure to *always* do and say those things that will assure your parents that—like Joseph Smith—you are a truthful teenager.

MOOSE ON THE TRAIL!

I belong to the National Ski Patrol and work at a nearby resort. One morning, I was asked to take a snowmobile to check conditions in a remote canyon. It was a busy day, and before I left my boss said, "Hustle back . . . we need that 'bile."

I quickly checked out the canyon, but while I was driving back, a young moose abruptly stepped from the trees and onto the trail in front of me. The next instant, the moose's mother walked onto the trail behind me.

Uh-oh, I thought, looking from one moose to the other. *This is going to be tricky . . .*

One place you *never* wanna be is between a young moose and its eight-hundred-pound mother.

I knew I couldn't—and shouldn't—try scaring them off the trail. And I knew that if I made any sudden moves, Mama Moose might actually attack. (I don't know what it's like to be stomped flat by a moose, and I didn't care to find out!)

I tried to radio up the mountain to tell my boss why I was being delayed, but I was in a radio "dead" zone. I tried my cell phone, but that wasn't working either.

In the end, the two moose kept me trapped for nearly half an hour before they wandered back into the trees. When I returned to patrol headquarters, my boss gave me a withering look.

But rather than yell or get mad, he simply lifted an eyebrow as if to say, "Okay, let's hear your story . . . and it better be good!"

I told him what happened, and he shook his head.

"That's the most ridiculous thing I've ever heard," he grumbled. And then in a slightly softer tone, he added, "If I'd heard it from anyone but you, I wouldn't have believed it."

A short time later I heard him repeating the story to another patroller. When the second man scoffed, my boss said, "You know Shane: if he said that's what happened, then that's what happened."

I was never sure what I had done to deserve that reputation. But I vowed then and there that I would never do anything to lose it.

FAMILY HOME EVENING

Joseph learned many things from Moroni. And he didn't keep them to himself. Moroni's messages were exciting and marvelous, and Joseph eagerly shared them with his family. "Every evening we gathered our children together and gave our time up to the discussion of those things [that Joseph learned]," his mother said. "I think that we presented the most peculiar aspect of any family that ever lived upon the earth, all seated in a circle . . . listening in breathless anxiety to the religious teachings of a boy eighteen years of age" (*The Revised and Enhanced History of Joseph Smith by His Mother* [Salt Lake City: Deseret Book, 1997], 111).

Sound like family home evening? It was! And according to Joseph's mother, those nightly gatherings filled their family with unity, happiness, and tranquility.

Wow!

Do you feel unity in your family? Happiness? Tranquility?

Having family home evening every week is one way to assure that you do.

Because you're a busy teenager, family home evening might sometimes interfere with sports, music, work, school, or any of the other activities you're involved with. But remember that whatever else is competing for your time, your *family* should always come first.

And so should family home evening.

"We cannot afford to neglect this heaven-inspired program," President Monson once said. "It can bring spiritual growth to each member of the family, helping him or her to withstand the temptations which are everywhere. The lessons learned in the home are those that last the longest" ("Constant Truths for Changing Times," *Ensign*, May 2005, 19).

Remember that successful family home evenings are up to you as much as your parents. So be sure to do more than simply show up. Support your parents by participating actively. Be enthusiastic, even if the activity isn't your idea of fun. Set an enthusiastic example for your brothers and sisters.

Keep in mind too that in Joseph's family, *he* was the one teaching the lessons. Can you imagine that? A teenage boy with little schooling keeping his family spellbound as he taught them? I'm sure that wasn't because Joseph was simply a naturally gifted teacher but because he was sincere and enthusiastic. You can be too. So when your turn comes to take charge or give a lesson, do it! And do it enthusiastically!

Remember that Joseph Smith could do it. And you can do it too.

DOING CHORES AND HELPING OUT

While we're on the subject of strengthening your family (and you might not want to hear this), Joseph Smith was always good about doing his chores. Even as an adult, Joseph chopped wood, lit fires, carried water, and tended the animals.

> Room kinda messy? Try spending ten minutes a day cleaning it. Yeah, it's only ten minutes, but in a week you'll have spent a whole *hour* on it!

Some people didn't believe that a prophet—the president of the Church—should stoop to such menial work. But when others actually said that to him, the Prophet quickly corrected them and then told them to follow his example.

Does that give you a new perspective on your own chores?

Joseph was also known for being careful with his tools, harnesses, and other farm equipment. He kept his plows and scythes sharpened, oiled, and neatly stored. He kept his yard trim and his house in good repair. Take a moment to picture your own bedroom. Do you keep it neat and orderly?

If not, learn a lesson from the Prophet Joseph!

> What family chore do you most dislike? Can you think of a way to make it more fun? Maybe playing music while you're washing dishes, "striping" the lawn when you mow it, taking your brother to a movie when you have to tend him . . .

FAMILY DUTY CHECKUP

Before we wrap things up, let's go through the checkup on the next page. Again, it's not a test, so relax and answer the questions the best you can, and skip any questions that don't apply to you.

Ready?

Go ahead!

FAMILY DUTY CHECKUP

Circle the number that best applies to you.

	I'M STRUGGLING				I'M AWESOME
I'm kind to everyone in my family:	1	2	3	4	5
I'm a good example for my brothers and sisters:	1	2	3	4	5
I'm good about doing my chores (without being asked):	1	2	3	4	5
I do my part to make family night successful:	1	2	3	4	5
I do my part to make family outings and activities more fun:	1	2	3	4	5
I support my parents (and I follow directions without whining):	1	2	3	4	5
I'm good about following family rules:	1	2	3	4	5
I'm good about sharing my life with my parents:	1	2	3	4	5
I'm a good sport when family activities are not my idea of "fun":	1	2	3	4	5
I keep my room and other belongings neat and orderly:	1	2	3	4	5
When I do my chores, I go the extra mile and do them the best that I can:	1	2	3	4	5

Okay, how'd that go? The purpose of the checkup wasn't to make you feel bad or guilty about anything. But take a good look at the numbers you circled. Do you notice anything? More important, do you see anything you could be better at? Anything you could do to help the family become more happy or unified?

Now you've found a great starting point for making your family even more awesome!

A swimming scuba diver is supported—or **buoyed up**—by air from his tank.

At the same time, he is **weighted down** by lead weights on his belt.

In your family, are you the force that buoys people up? Or are you the weight that brings them down?

Which *should* you be?

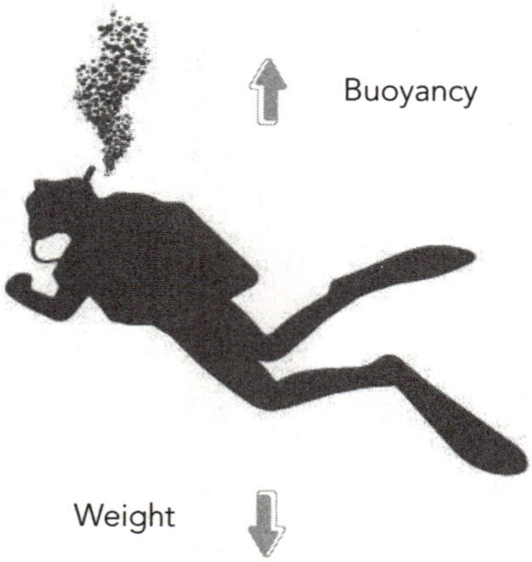

FINALLY

After Moroni's first visit, Joseph sat back on his bed, marveling over his experience. But minutes later, a light suddenly appeared in the room, and there was Moroni again.

And the angel repeated his entire message.

I don't know what Joseph thought when Moroni began repeating himself. But then Moroni appeared again and repeated his message a *third* time!

And the next day? After Joseph's father sent him home to rest, Moroni appeared and repeated the whole thing . . . for the fourth time!

The *fourth* time!

Have you ever wondered about that? About why Moroni had to appear again . . . and again . . . and again?

I'm sure it's partly because Moroni's message was so important that it needed to be emphasized. Moroni needed to be absolutely *certain* that Joseph understood what he was being taught. And by repeating his message, he planted it firmly into the young prophet's mind.

And let me promise you something: when Moroni began repeating himself for the second, third, and fourth time, the one thing Joseph *didn't* do was stretch, yawn, and say, "Yeah, yeah . . . you already said that!"

No, he *listened* . . . and he listened hard!

He listened as if he were hearing it all for the first time.

Now, there will be times when your parents, teachers, and other adults repeat themselves to you too. (Did you just nod vigorously? Yeah, I thought so!) Trust me, it will happen again . . . and again and again.

But when it does, remember that it's not because anyone thinks you're unable to remember anything. Some things just need to be repeated. So be a good sport. Remember that Joseph Smith needed to hear things more than once. And if it was necessary for him, it might be necessary for you, too.

So far, I've talked a lot about Joseph Smith's experiences with his family, but let me talk about *you* for a minute. Flex your fingers, take a deep breath, then try the discovery on the next two pages. As always, we're just trying to discover a few things about yourself, so relax and try to have a little fun as you answer the questions.

All set?

Let's do it.

GREAT FAMILY DISCOVERY!

Think of a really awesome family you know. Who are they?

What sort of things make that family so "great"? Do they get along well? Do lots of fun things? Succeed at sports, or music, or school? Think it over and try to come up with at least three things.

Is there anything you could do to develop one of those qualities in *your* family?

(Give it some thought now! If you really put some effort into it, what could *your* family be known for?)

What's one thing you could do *today* to help develop that quality in your family? (Hey . . . go do it!)

How could you follow your friend's example to make *your* family even more special? What do *they* do that *you* could do too? Why not give it a try!

Do you have a friend who has a terrific family? What sort of things does your friend do to help make their family so incredible?

What could you do today to develop that quality even more? (Let's get out there now and do it!)

Is there anything that makes *your* family "stand out" in your ward or neighborhood? Something that makes your family unique or special? What is it?

Wow! If you're like me, you now have a couple of good, concrete ideas for blessing your family. But none of them will do any good unless you follow through and put them to work. So do it!

Your relationship with your family is one of the most important things you'll ever develop in this life. So follow Joseph Smith's example and make your family a priority. Talk with your parents often. Be truthful. Be enthusiastic about family home evening. And be patient if your parents need to repeat themselves from time to time.

Who knows? Maybe one day your own kids will do the same for you!

ACTION STEPS!

Final ideas for helping out your family:

Think about your last family night. On a scale of 1 to 5, how well did you contribute?

1 2 3 4 5

What could you have done to make the evening more successful?

When you do your chores, do you do them quickly (or even sloppily) just to get them done? Or do you do your best work? Give yourself a grade:

A B C D F

(How should you be doing them?)

Go have a talk with your parents. Right now! It doesn't matter what you talk about, but just talk! Make sure your lines of communication are open.

Do you have a chore you haven't done yet today? (Hey, I'm glad you're reading my book, but go get your chores done! And try to have a little fun with it!)

THREE

DRESSING FOR THE DANCE

BUILDING BONDS WITH YOUR BROTHERS AND SISTERS

Sixteen-year-old Stephen Hamilton strutted into the kitchen like a Hollywood star on his first trip down the red carpet.

"Well," he said, striking a masculine pose. "What do you think?"

His older sister began laughing. But then—catching the look on Steve's face—she quickly caught herself.

"Oh," she said. "You're not *trying* to be funny?"

Steve looked down at his clothes. "You don't think this looks good?"

Michelle thought fast. Her younger brother had just turned sixteen. He was the youngest, freshest, most newly minted priest in the Church, on his way to his first school dance.

The only problem was that Steve understood fashion about as well as he understood Klingon . . . and he wasn't a Star Trek fan.

"Your shirt clashes with your T-shirt," she said, trying not to sound too harsh. "And those jeans . . . "

She shook her head sadly.

Steve cast a panicked look at the clock. "Jon's picking me up in half an hour! What am I gonna do?"

"C'mon," she said, taking him by the hand. "We've still got time."

Michelle marched into Steve's bedroom and tore into his closet like a puppy after a bone.

"Now this is a casual dance, right?" she asked over her shoulder.

Steve ducked as a pair of basketball shoes flew past his head.

"Yeah . . ."

"So no ties or anything?"

"No . . . just nice, school-kind of clothes."

"Ugh!"—Michelle held up a mildewing basketball jersey—"*Really*?"

"Please yell at me later," Steve pleaded. "For now, just help me!"

Michelle left the closet and attacked the dresser. "Oh! Okay," she said almost instantly. "Now we're in business."

She handed her brother a pair of black jeans. "Go put these on."

"These?"

"Steve!"

"*Ohh-kaay.*"

> Has a brother or sister ever done something really cool for you?
>
> How did that make you feel?
>
> Is there something you could do to make *them* feel the same way?
>
> Why not go do it now?

By the time Steve had changed into the fresh jeans, Michelle had a shirt and T-shirt ready. "These shirts complement each other," she explained. "They're both nice, but together they're fantastic!"

Steve pulled on the shirts and checked them in the mirror.

"Tuck in the T-shirt," Michelle instructed, "but leave the other shirt out and unbuttoned."

Steve did as he was told, and Michelle looked him over like a Marine Corps general inspecting an awkward recruit. "Looking good," she announced. "Just one more thing . . ."

She took him into the bathroom and grabbed a hairbrush.

"Michelle, no—"

"Steve, your hair's too forced—"

"*Forced*?"

"Yeah, it's too George McFly—"

"George . . . ?"

"George McFly? *Back to the Future*? Oh, never mind. Now just relax!"

With the focus of a surgeon performing a delicate procedure, Michelle made a few adjustments to her brother's hair and said, "Now *that* looks good!"

Steve looked into the mirror. "Wow! That *does* look good!"

Michelle checked her watch. "Don't get a big head. Now you'd better get going."

"I couldn't believe what happened that night," Steve said when he shared his experience. "The first girl I saw that night said, 'Wow, you look *good* tonight!' "

And she wasn't the only one. While Steve's friends didn't say much—"I think they were jealous!" Steve said—a lot of the young women oohed and awed over him.

(Steve was so jazzed that the next day he repaid his sister by washing and waxing her car.)

I've always admired brothers and sisters who get along with one another. And I can't think of anything cooler than being best friends with your own brothers and sisters.

And I know many young people who are.

You see, there are few things in this world—or in the Church—that are as important as your family. There are few people you should be closer to than your parents, brothers, and sisters.

I used to have a twelve-year-old boy named Jason on my baseball team. Besides being a great ballplayer, Jason was a natural team leader and one of the most popular young men in his school.

But what really impressed me was Jason's commitment to his family.

One day our team had just finished practice when one of the boys suggested going to the ballpark to watch a rival team play. Everyone was instantly enthusiastic. But before leaving, Jason came running over to ask the time.

"Almost five o'clock," I said.

"Oh, hey, I can't go," Jason told his friends. "My sister's got a softball game."

Jason's friends knew him well enough not to try talking him out of going, but I wanted to know more.

"You go to all of your sister's games?" I asked.

He nodded matter-of-factly. "She comes to mine," he said.

As I got to know Jason better, I found that he wasn't kidding. His brothers and sisters did go to his games, and he went to theirs.

I thought it was impressive that attending his sister's games was more important to him than hanging out with his friends.

And that's something Joseph Smith understood before he ever walked into the Sacred Grove.

You might have heard about when Joseph was seven and had an infection in his leg. (We'll talk about it in the next chapter.) When people tell that story, they usually focus on Joseph's incredible courage.

But there was another hero there. Joseph's older brother Hyrum—just twelve years old at the time—often sat beside him for hours, squeezing Joseph's leg to ease the pain. According to their mother, Hyrum once sat beside his little brother twenty-four hours a day for more than a week.

Can you imagine the bond that formed between the two after that? It was the sort of thing that later prompted Joseph to say, "I love [Hyrum] with that love that is stronger than death" (*History of the Church*, 2:338).

And for Joseph and Hyrum, those weren't just fancy words. Over and over again they showed how close true brothers could be. When Joseph went to Carthage, for instance—knowing he would be killed—he begged Hyrum not to go. He pleaded with him to return home, to his family, where he would be safe.

Hyrum simply shook his head. "Joseph, I can't leave you."

But to me, the most touching example of their brotherly bond occurred just a few days before.

A month earlier, the Nauvoo city council had destroyed the press of an anti-Mormon newspaper. Mobsters were screaming for blood, clamoring for Joseph's head. They threatened to tear Nauvoo apart to find him.

The members of your family are like the links of a chain, which is only as strong as its weakest link. There may be times when a struggling brother or sister is that weak link. (Joseph Smith, Nephi, and others all had siblings that created occasional challenges!)

Be sure that *you* are always a strong link! Be there to strengthen your brothers and sisters when they need it!

After much prayer, Joseph decided to leave Illinois until things calmed down. After all, he was the one the mob wanted. And if he was away, the mobs would have no reason to bother the people of Nauvoo.

Have you ever asked a brother or sister for help or advice?

How did it feel knowing they were there for you? (Are you always helpful when your brothers and sisters need you? Can you do better?)

He didn't *want* to leave, of course. Going away meant leaving his wife and children—not to mention his home and friends—to live in the wilderness. But it was the only way to protect the city . . . and the people.

It was a good plan. But as Joseph and Hyrum were preparing to leave, they were accosted by men who accused them of being afraid.

"Running away looks cowardly," one man said. "It's not what men do."

"Cowardly?" Joseph couldn't have been more shocked if he'd been struck by lightning. He was stunned; the accusation cut through him like a knife. "Cowardly?"

"You always said you'd stand by us," another man said. "But now that the wolves are upon us, you're leaving the flock to be devoured."

"Is that what you think?" Hyrum asked, standing up for his brother. "Joseph's not leaving for his sake. He's leaving for the good of the people! He's leaving to protect the people!"

President Ezra Taft Benson once said: "Remember, the family is one of God's greatest fortresses against the evils of our day. Help keep your family strong and close and worthy of our Father in Heaven's blessings. As you do, you will receive faith and strength which will bless your lives forever" ("To the 'Youth of the Noble Birthright,' " *Ensign*, May 1986, 43).

Joseph was still too stunned to speak. And to make matters worse, his wife Emma had written a letter, begging him not to leave.

I can't begin to imagine the frustration Joseph felt at that moment. I can't imagine the disappointment. He was willing to leave everything—his family, his home, his friends—to ensure the safety of Nauvoo and the Saints who lived there. But the very people he was trying to protect were accusing him of cowardice.

Joseph was overwhelmed with confusion and frustration. He knew he'd be killed if he went to Carthage. But he couldn't bear to have people thinking he was a coward.

For one of the few times in his life, Joseph didn't know what to do. He was overcome with disappointment and uncertainty. And in that awful moment of darkness and despair, he did an amazing thing.

He turned to his older brother for help.

"Brother Hyrum," he said, "you are the oldest . . . What should I do?"

I've often thought about that moment . . . and I've always been touched by it. Joseph Smith—the man who saw and spoke with God the Eternal Father and his son Jesus Christ.

The man who talked with Moroni.

The man who talked with John the Baptist, Elias, and the apostles Peter, James, and John.

The man chosen by God to restore his Church to the earth.

When Joseph was overwhelmed with grief and despair, whom did he turn to for help?

His older brother.

Wow.

Now, wouldn't it be great if *you* had brothers or sisters you could turn to when times were tough? Maybe you do. If so, I hope you appreciate them!

But more important, are you that kind of a brother or sister yourself?

If you're not, *you can be!*

Take a look at the following discovery for ways to get started.

BEING A GREAT BROTHER OR SISTER

Place a mark on the line that best describes you. How good are you at being a great brother or sister?

Not so much Absolutely!

____

Now, just for fun, go back and put a mark where you think your brothers and sisters would put you!

Big question: Why do you think they'd put you there? We're all friends here, so be honest now! Are you less committed than you should be?

Are you selfish?

Bossy?

Insensitive?

C'mon . . . what is it?

Think of one thing you could do *today* that would allow you to put your own mark a little farther to the right.

What is it?

(And why not go do it now?)

Have you ever seen one of your siblings' eyeballs pop?

Wanna give it a try?

Go right now and do their least favorite chore for them!

Seriously!

(And when they ask why you did that, just smile and say, "'Cause you're my fave!")

Give it a try!

While Joseph Smith was translating the plates, his brother Samuel sometimes did his chores for him, giving Joseph more time to translate.

What could you do to help or support one of your siblings? (And if you don't have brothers or sisters, use a parent, friend, neighbor, or relative.)

Now, take a minute and go do it!

When Joseph was seven and suffering with an abscess in his leg, Hyrum often sat beside him for hours, squeezing the leg to ease the pain.

Is there anything you could do right now for a brother, sister, or parent having a tough time? (Go do it!)

Choose one of your brothers or sisters (you get extra credit if it's someone you might not always get along with). Now, can you think of something you could do today to cheer them up, help them out, or brighten their day? What is it?

Go do it!

All done?

Great!

You now have a couple of ideas for forging better, stronger relationships with your brothers and sisters. But you have to follow through!

Do something for them *today*!

And don't be afraid to ask for their help in return. Little acts of give and take will do wonders in building a bond of love and friendship.

There was a time when Joseph Smith had a disagreement with his younger brother William. It was a touchy situation, but William made things even worse by stirring up problems behind Joseph's back. He openly criticized Joseph, telling people that his brother was a fallen prophet.

William was so angry that he even managed to turn their brother Samuel against Joseph too.

Boy, wouldn't that make family dinner a little uncomfortable?

I don't know how you might have handled a situation like that. But the Prophet Joseph was patient. He loved his little brother and refused to give up on him. He said that he would do whatever it took to work things out. And he was true to his word. Following the Lord's counsel to show an "increase in love" (D&C 121:43), he worked, prayed, and showed even more love for William.

In time, William responded. It didn't happen overnight, but eventually the two forgave one another and became friends again.

If you have a strained relationship with a brother or sister, it might take time to work out the wrinkles. But don't let that discourage you. Follow the Prophet Joseph's example and be patient. And be sure that you do your part to work things out.

And whatever you do, don't ever, *ever* give up!

Finally, make your brothers and sisters a priority in your life.

"In a world of turmoil and uncertainty," Elder L. Tom Perry once said, "it is more important than ever to make our families the center of our lives and the top of our priorities. Families lie at the center of our Heavenly Father's plan" ("The Importance of the Family," *Ensign,* May 2003, 40).

"The center of our lives."

"The top of our priorities."

Did you catch that?

We've already seen examples of the bonds between Joseph and Hyrum. But those bonds extended to other members of the family too. The Prophet's younger brother Samuel, for instance, took over many of Joseph's chores, chopping wood, plowing fields, and harvesting crops to give his brother more time to translate the gold plates.

Later, when Samuel heard Joseph and Hyrum were in danger in Carthage Jail, he jumped into a wagon and raced to help them. He was attacked by a mob on the way, ducking bullets as he raced into the woods, barely getting away.

But his narrow escape didn't stop him. His older brothers were in trouble, and he was determined to help. He charged home, found a fresh horse, and once again raced for Carthage.

This time he made it, but it was too late. Joseph and Hyrum had already been killed. Samuel was the first Latter-day Saint to reach them. And he was the one who put their bodies in a wagon and drove them back to Nauvoo.

It was a final act of love from a devoted younger brother.

The Lord has said to "strengthen your brethren in all your conversation, in all your prayers, in all your exhortations, and in all your doings" (D&C 108:7).

He also said to "succor the weak, lift up the hands which hang down, and strengthen the feeble knees" (D&C 81:5).

Waz that mean?

It means to help others, to encourage them when they're down, to lift them up when they're discouraged, to guide them when they're confused, to be there when they need a friend.

You can do all those things for other people. But you should **start at home**! Remember that the members of your family are here to lift, support, and help one another.

Be sure that you're doing *your* part!

Remember that your Heavenly Father placed you in your family for a reason. Your parents, brothers, and sisters are not random people you merely happen to live with. They're an important part of your life. And they really are special.

So do your part to make your family one that the Lord will be proud of. Truly make it the center of your life and the top of your priorities!

BEING A GREAT SIBLING CHECKUP

Suppose your brothers and sisters got together and gave you a report card. How would they grade you on each of the following?

Seeing the best in them (no matter how goofy they get):	A	B	C	D	F
Supporting them (no matter what crazy things they're up to):	A	B	C	D	F
Spending time with them (even if they only want to play Candyland):	A	B	C	D	F
Sharing with them (even if it's your favorite CD):	A	B	C	D	F
Including them in activities (and pretending to not be embarrassed being seen with them):	A	B	C	D	F
Helping out around the house (and smiling as you do!):	A	B	C	D	F

Having a good attitude (especially when times are tough):	A	B	C	D	F
Being a good listener (no matter how silly their problems are):	A	B	C	D	F
Being a peacemaker (after all, the Lord would rather have peace in the family than see you win the argument):	A	B	C	D	F
Supporting your parents (hey, they've got a pretty hard job, here!):	A	B	C	D	F
Being a good example (you know your brothers and sisters are watching you!)	A	B	C	D	F
Making the family stronger (after all, you're all in this together):	A	B	C	D	F
Helping other family members feel important ('cause don't you want them to do the same for you?):	A	B	C	D	F

Well . . . how did that go? (I hope you're getting good grades!)

But now, choose an item from the list you might not have earned an "A" in. What is it?

And what's one thing you could do *right now* to improve your grade in that area

Now . . . go do it!

I used to live near a young woman named Darcy. And as I'd go around the neighborhood, I often saw her on the front lawn with her little sisters, all of them dressed up with cute skirts and pom-poms, doing cheerleading routines.

"What's going on?" I asked one day as I was walking my dog.

"Cheerleading camp!" Darcy exclaimed.

And then (turning to her sisters): "Ready? Oh-kaay! We're the best in all the street, we're so good we can't be beat . . ."

And on and on they went, yelling, jumping, and waving their pom-poms like they were being attacked by bees.

I later found out that Darcy was only babysitting. But when Darcy tended, she didn't simply plop her sisters in front of the TV and tell them not to bother her.

She played with them!

More than that, she turned them into the most enthusiastic, energetic, cute-as-buttons cheerleaders in the neighborhood (and became even closer to them as she did).

FOUR

SKI PATROL COMING THROUGH!

FOLLOWING JOSEPH SMITH'S EXAMPLE OF COURAGE

"Base patrol, seven forty-seven."

"Base patrol."

"I need a snowmobile assist in the skiway, five minutes."

"Ten-four. It's on its way."

I released the radio button and put my hand back on the toboggan handle, turning my skis and braking in the snow. Trying to move as smoothly as possible, I pointed my skis downhill for a moment and then hit the brakes again, keeping myself from going too fast.

It was Saturday, and I was working as a ski patrolman in Park City, Utah. A few minutes earlier, a fourteen-year-old boy named Brandon had taken a nasty spill, breaking his leg. I'd helped to splint his leg and was now towing him in a toboggan to the resort clinic at the bottom of the mountain.

I usually enjoyed this part of the job. I liked helping people, and towing toboggans was fun. But not today. Brandon's leg was in bad shape, and he was in a lot of pain. His injury was severe enough that I'd called ahead for an ambulance. And I was doing my best to keep the ride as smooth as possible while I skied him down the hill.

The hill flattened and the toboggan bogged down in the soft snow. On most days patrolmen could skate through the flat spot. But today the snow was so mushy that I'd called ahead for help: a snowmobile was waiting there for me.

I slid up to the machine and clipped a rope to the toboggan.

"Okay . . . let's go!"

The driver, a patroller named Syd, eased the 'bile ahead until we were moving smoothly and then accelerated across the flat.

"Ski Patrol," she called out, standing on the running boards so she could see over the crowds. "Coming through!"

Syd weaved the snowmobile expertly through the crowds until we reached the clinic at the bottom of the mountain. Four patrollers were outside waiting for us.

"Hey, guys," I said, stepping out of my skis and trying to sound cheerful. "This is Brandon. He's got a lower leg fracture and he's in a lot of pain."

The patrollers responded energetically as they descended upon the injured boy, releasing the straps and tarps that secured him in the toboggan.

"Hi, Brandon!"

"Hey, there, bud!"

"Not having such a good day, huh?"

I followed as the patrolmen lifted the litter and carried Brandon into the clinic. One patroller took Brandon's pulse while another examined the splint on his leg. Once inside the clinic, they set the litter down.

I pulled off my gloves and goggles and knelt beside the injured boy.

"Hey, kiddo . . . are you hanging in there?"

Brandon's face was chalky, his eyes filled with tears. "Yes."

"You're doing great, bud. Your parents should be here any minute, and we've got an ambulance on the way."

" 'Kay."

I patted him reassuringly, wishing there was something more I could do for him. Despite the pain, Brandon had been extraordinarily brave throughout his ordeal. He bit his lip, and tears trickled down his cheeks.

Within minutes an ambulance arrived, but Brandon grabbed my hand before the paramedics wheeled him away.

"Thank you," he whispered.

I smiled and patted his shoulder. "Anytime."

I couldn't help admiring Brandon's courage. And while I watched the ambulance drive away, I was thinking of another boy who'd been brave in the face of excruciating pain.

When Joseph Smith was seven years old, an abscess formed in his leg. It hurt so much that his brother Hyrum often sat beside him for hours to comfort him and squeeze his leg to ease the pain. There wasn't any cure, and Joseph's doctor believed the only option was to amputate the leg.

But there was a doctor nearby who'd developed a new technique. His name was Nathan Smith, and his procedure was so new, and so radical, historians believe he was the only physician in the world at the time who could have performed it.

> Can you imagine going to the dentist to have a tooth drilled—or pulled—without laughing gas? Without anything to deaden the pain? What would that be like?

Was it a coincidence that he lived within riding distance of Joseph Smith's home?

I don't think so.

At any rate, Dr. Smith proposed cutting out the diseased portions of the young boy's bone. And Joseph's parents agreed to let him try.

Unlike today, there was no anesthetic to put Joseph to sleep during the operation. And so to keep him from jerking or thrashing about, Dr. Smith wanted to tie him to the bed.

Joseph shook his head.

"No," he said. "I'll keep still. You won't need to tie me."

> Try to imagine what young Joseph was about to go through. Try to imagine being seven years old, surrounded by doctors who were going to cut into your leg . . . and without anything to ease the pain.

Dr. Smith was skeptical. He suggested that Joseph drink a little brandy or wine to dull the pain. Remember that this was before the Word of Wisdom; the Lord had not yet revealed the dangers of alcohol.

But Joseph refused anyway.

"No," he said. "I won't do that. But if you'll let my father sit on the bed and hold me, I promise I'll keep still."

I hope you can appreciate what was about to happen. I can't even *begin* to imagine the pain and horror the young boy was about to face.

Father Smith wrapped his son in his arms and held him tightly.

Dr. Smith took a deep breath and then sliced into Joseph's leg, cutting deeply enough to expose the bone.

With crude tools, he drilled holes into the bone; he then used a knife to carve grooves between the holes, forming a rectangle.

And then, using strong forceps, he snapped off the chunk of infected bone.

Joseph cried out in pain. His mother heard him and came flying into the room to find her son's face covered with sweat, his bed soaked with blood. Joseph begged her to leave, not wanting her to see him suffer.

Despite his own pain and agony, he was more worried about his mother than himself.

And the doctor was only getting started. He had to repeat the procedure several more times until he'd removed every bit of infected bone.

It was an excruciating operation. And Joseph endured it with nothing more than his father's loving arms to comfort him.

Joseph eventually recovered, though he lost so much weight that for months his mother was able to carry him around as easily as a sack of apples. When his family moved to Palmyra, New York, two years later, Joseph walked most of the way, hobbling along on his crutches.

Even though Joseph was only a boy, he was already showing examples of the courage that would mark his life.

"Courage [was] one of Joseph Smith's special qualities," Elder Neal A. Maxwell once said. "Without it, he would have shrunk from carrying out his remarkable role" (" 'My Servant Joseph,' " *Ensign*, May 1992, 37).

And Elder Maxwell was right. Joseph's life was marked not only by great achievements but by tremendous trials, challenges, and disappointments too. But he stood fast through it all, displaying extraordinary bravery and courage.

One of the most dramatic examples of Joseph's steadfastness occurred when he was fourteen and walked into a grove of trees to offer a heartfelt prayer. Afterwards, he courageously stood his ground when he was ridiculed and persecuted for telling his story.

And he never denied what he knew to be true.

"I was hated and persecuted for saying that I had seen a vision," he wrote, "yet it was true; and while they were persecuting me, reviling me, and speaking all manner of evil against me falsely for so saying, I was led to say in my heart: Why persecute me for telling the truth? I have actually seen a vision; and who am I that I can withstand God, or why does the whole world think to make me deny what I have actually seen? For I had seen a vision; I knew it, and I knew that God knew it, and I could not deny it, neither dared I do it; at least I knew that by so doing I would offend God, and come under condemnation" (Joseph Smith—History 1:25).

Was it hard for Joseph to tell his story?

Of course it was!

Did it hurt when people ridiculed him for it?

Absolutely!

Did that stop him from doing what was right?

Of course not!

Though people mocked and abused him for it, Joseph went about his Heavenly Father's business and "heeded them not" (1 Nephi 8:33).

President Thomas S. Monson once said, "Step by step, facing opposition at nearly every turn and yet always guided by the hand of the Lord, Joseph organized The Church of Jesus Christ of Latter-day Saints. He proved courageous in all that he did" ("Models to Follow," *Ensign*, Nov. 2002, 62).

Now, times are different than they were for Joseph Smith. You face temptations, dangers, and challenges that didn't even exist in the early days of the Church. But Joseph's remarkable courage can nevertheless be an example to you.

> Suppose one of your friends began using foul language or telling inappropriate stories. What could you do—or say—to change the mood, or to shift the conversation in a more positive direction?

When Joseph was imprisoned in Richmond, Missouri, his jailers began telling horrible and disgusting tales. Lying next to the Prophet, Parley P. Pratt became so horrified that he was about to rebuke them. But before he could act, Joseph rose to his feet and with "a voice of thunder" cried, "Silence, ye fiends of the infernal pit! In the name of Jesus Christ I rebuke you, and command you to be still; I will not live another minute and hear such language. Cease such talk, or you or I die this instant!"

According to Brother Pratt, Joseph then "ceased to speak. He stood erect in terrible majesty. Chained and without a weapon; calm, unruffled and dignified as an angel, he looked upon the quailing guards, whose weapons were lowered or dropped to the ground; whose knees smote together, and who, shrinking into a corner, or crouching at his feet, begged his pardon, and remained quiet till a change of guards" (*Autobiography of Parley P. Pratt* [Salt Lake City: Deseret Book, 1985], 210–211).

That was a bold example of Joseph standing up for what was right. But things don't always have to be so dramatic.

> Have you ever seen someone choose the right in a difficult situation?
>
> How did that feel?
>
> What did you think of that person? (And would you like people to think of *you* that way?)

I have a young friend named Abram who was once riding a bus with his high school football team. As the boys joked and kidded with one another, a lively discussion became crude and offensive.

Not liking the tone the conversation was taking, Abram suddenly said, "Hey, Andy . . . you gonna keep your shoes on tonight?"

The whole team burst into howls, everyone turning to look at the team kicker, who was turning the color of a ripe cherry. The previous game, Andy had kicked the ball so hard his shoe had flown off.

"Yeah!" another player chimed in. "You're the only kicker in the state to score a field goal with your *shoe*!"

The kicker was suddenly the focus of everyone's good-natured ribbing. And just that fast the ugliness was gone. With a single question—and without any preaching or moralizing—Abram changed something bad into something good.

You can do the same thing.

Yes, it might be hard. And yes, it might be scary. But when you're faced with a choice, you can—like Joseph Smith—muster your courage and do what's right.

TV DETECTIVE

If you've ever watched one of those high-tech crime shows on TV, you know you can't go anywhere without leaving some kind of evidence that you were there. No matter how careful you are, you're bound to leave a fingerprint, a fiber from your clothes, or a speck of dirt from your shoes.

In the same way, you can't interact with others without a bit of your attitude or personality rubbing off a little. The question is, what kind of "evidence" are you leaving behind?

Do you leave people feeling optimistic?

Encouraged?

Energized?

Happy?

Hopeful?

Courageous?

And what about situations?

Do you leave situations better than you found them?

If a situation turns ugly, do you do your best to change it?

Do you always "choose the right?" (And let the consequence follow?)

Do you stand up for others?

Stand up for your friends?

Stand up for your beliefs?

Stand up for what's **right**?

You never know who's watching you.

You never know what effect your actions, words, and attitudes will have on someone else.

Be sure that you always leave "**good evidence**" behind!

> "The call for courage comes constantly to each of us," President Monson once said. "It has ever been so, and so shall it ever be" ("The Call for Courage," *Ensign*, May 2004, 54).

I know a young man named Joel who was going through a tough time at school. A group of older boys continually teased, harassed, and frightened him.

The older boys weren't really bad kids, but they didn't realize how much they were hurting the younger boy. One day a boy named Zach was standing with them when Joel came walking down the hall. As the older boys began their cruel taunts, Zach saw the hurt in Joel's eyes. And he spoke up.

"Knock it off, guys," he said quietly.

And then—turning to Joel—he said, "Come on . . . I'll walk you to class."

With tears in his eyes, Joel told me that the older kids never bothered him again.

Zach didn't make a fuss that day. He didn't cause a commotion, and he didn't make a scene. But his actions blessed a life.

You, too, can summon the courage to choose the right, even when it's difficult or frightening.

Try this: Read through the following situations and try to decide how Joseph Smith might have handled each of them. (If you're not sure, try to imagine what the Savior might do, or President Monson, or someone you admire from school.)

But don't cheat! And don't skip any situations! Take a moment to think up an answer to each one, even if it's something you don't think applies to you. Doing this will get your creative juices flowing and condition you to think up solutions when you need them.

Ready? Let's give it a try!

SITUATION DISCOVERY!

What do you think the Prophet Joseph would do if someone

- began using foul language?
- began telling off-color stories?

- wanted to watch an inappropriate movie?
- was wearing immodest clothing?
- began teasing someone at school?
- tried shoplifting?
- wanted to cheat on a test?
- tried cutting in line at the movies?
- began complaining about the next Mutual activity?
- began whining about the bishop or your Sunday School or seminary teacher?
- wanted to skip a class?
- began gossiping about someone at school?

That's quite a list! (I hope you never have to deal with all those things!) But if you worked your way through every situation, seriously thinking up solutions, you probably came up with a few ideas. You began "conditioning" yourself to think up ideas, which will help when a situation requiring courage comes up.

"Let us have the courage to defy the consensus, the courage to stand for principle," President Monson said. "Courage, not compromise, brings the smile of God's approval" ("The Call for Courage," *Ensign*, May 2004, 54).

The next time you're in a situation that requires courage, remember the words of the song, "Do What is Right." Remember the Prophet Joseph's courage in making the right decisions . . . and then do the same thing!

President Spencer W. Kimball was once in the hospital to undergo open-heart surgery. As his bed was being wheeled toward the operating room, an attendant smashed his finger in the door. That had to hurt, of course. And the young man took the Savior's name in vain. Though he was sedated, President Kimball managed to open his eyes and say, "Young man, don't say that; He's my best friend!" (quoted by Robert E. Wells, "Be a Friend, a Servant, a Son of the Savior," *Ensign*, Nov. 1982, 69).

ACTION STEPS!

Think of a time when *you* needed personal courage to "do what is right."

Did you choose the right?

Are you happy with your actions? If not, is there something else you could have done?

Would you handle the situation differently if it happened again?

(Is there anything you learned from your first experience that would make things easier?)

Have you ever seen a good friend or leader choose the right in a tough situation?

What did they do?

How did it make you feel to see them do that?

(Is their example one you'd like to follow? Why?)

Could you do the same thing in a similar situation?

Find a sticky note (or a note card) and write President Monson's thought, "Courage Counts," on it. Use it to remind you of Joseph Smith's example the next time you need a boost of courage.

FIVE TRAGEDY IN CARTHAGE

CHOOSING THE RIGHT WHEN THE CHOICE IS HARD

"A poor wayfaring man of grief
Hath often crossed me on my way,
Who sued so humbly for relief
That I could never answer nay."

Brother Sanders—my tenth-grade Seminary teacher—was standing at the front of the room dressed in an old-fashioned shirt and vest, a gold chain looping from a pocket. He was staring across the room as if looking into eternity as he sang.

"I had not pow'r to ask his name,
Where-to he went, or whence he came;
Yet there was something in his eye
That won my love; I knew not why."

Brother Sanders had a rich, baritone voice that blended perfectly with the haunting lyrics and melody of the hymn. He mesmerized the class with his performance.

"Then in a moment to my view
The stranger started from disguise.
The tokens in his hands I knew;
The Savior stood before mine eyes."

The class was silent as Brother Sanders sang. I'd heard the song before—it was one of my favorites—but I felt chills as his voice trailed off . . . and he whispered the final stanza.

"He spake and my poor name he named,
'Of me thou hast not been ashamed.
These deeds shall they memorial be;
Fear not, thou didst them unto me.' "
("A Poor Wayfaring Man of Grief," *Hymns*, no. 29)

Brother Sanders' voice faded away, and he looked around as if noticing for the first time that a roomful of students was watching him.

"Carthage Jail," he said. "John Taylor and Willard Richards were in an upper room with Joseph and Hyrum Smith. John Taylor sang that song. When he finished, Hyrum asked him to sing it again."

The teacher nodded solemnly. And then he told us about the mob storming the two-story building.

About the bullets smashing through the walls and the windows.

About the guards pretending to defend the prisoners, firing blank shots into the air as the mob rushed past.

About the swarm of men smashing through the doors, pounding up the stairs, and attempting to break into the prisoners' room.

About Willard Richards using his cane to knock away the musket barrels being shoved past the door.

About John Taylor being shot . . . and then shot again, and again, and again.

With tears in his eyes, he told us about the bullet smashing through the door and striking Hyrum in the face.

And he told us about Joseph leaping from the window, being shot four times as he fell.

> Close your eyes and try to imagine being in Carthage Jail with Joseph Smith. Try to imagine the noise, the commotion, and the confusion. Try to imagine the shouts of the mob and the roar of the rifles. What would it have been like to be there?

I'd heard the story before. But listening to Brother Sanders, I felt as if I was actually there, actually watching the awful events while they happened.

But Brother Sanders paused after a moment, looking toward the back of the room.

"Ethan?" he asked. "You have a . . . *look* on your face."

My friend Ethan looked up, obviously embarrassed.

"Oh, no," he said, just a little too quickly. "It's nothing."

"It's okay," Brother Sanders assured him. "Tell us what you're thinking."

Ethan hesitated, then said, "Okay, I appreciate what you're saying. And I don't want to ruin the spirit . . ."

"But . . ." the teacher prompted.

"Well," Ethan finally said, "why did Joseph jump from the window? I mean, I don't want to say this, but wasn't that kind of cowardly?"

A gasp went up from the class, and one girl even said, "Ethan!"

"No, no, that's okay," Brother Sanders said. He smiled kindly. "I certainly wasn't there, Ethan. But I'll tell you what I think."

The teacher turned and walked to the window, gesturing outside. "There was an angry mob out there," he said as if actually seeing the raging crowd. "Hundreds of armed men with their faces painted to look like Indians; so many rifles firing that the gunshots sounded like a long, single crack of thunder; bullets peppering the jail and gun smoke filling the air."

He turned to look at Ethan. "Do you think Joseph had *any* chance of getting away?"

"No."

"I don't think so either. And I don't think Joseph thought so. He knew there was no way out. Hyrum had been killed. John Taylor had been shot four times. . . . Joseph had to know it was only a matter of seconds before Taylor and Richards were both killed."

A strange look crossed Ethan's face. "You mean Joseph was trying to *save* them?"

Brother Sanders shrugged, "I wasn't there—"

"But what do you *think?*"

"Joseph could see the mob in the square," a young woman named Kelsey pointed out. "He could see the men out there waiting for him. He *knew* he didn't have a chance."

"And the second he jumped, the men rushing the bedroom ran back outside," someone else reminded us. "That gave Willard Richards time to drag John Taylor into the next room and hide him in the straw."

I could see tears in Ethan's eyes. "So he jumped to save their lives?"

"Willard Richards believed he did," Brother Sanders said.

He paused for a moment before continuing. "Joseph sealed his testimony with his blood. And I believe that he gave his life for his friends."

Everyone in the room had been teary-eyed before. But several kids were now crying openly. I remember having such a huge lump in my throat that it hurt.

I went home that afternoon with a better understanding of that awful day in Carthage. I appreciated Joseph and Hyrum even more for their sacrifice. And I had no question that when Joseph Smith faced tough, difficult decisions, he acted courageously.

Is there something *you* could be more courageous at?

Something like attending your meetings, resisting temptations, or avoiding inappropriate music, video games, or movies? Sharing the gospel with nonmembers? Living the Word of Wisdom?

How could the Prophet Joseph's example help you with that?

President Monson said that "Joseph Smith taught us courage—by example" ("The Prophet Joseph Smith: Teacher by Example," *Ensign*, Nov. 2005, 67).

And he was right. The Prophet Joseph faced many tough decisions in his life, and he showed remarkable courage making them.

The night before Joseph was martyred, for instance, a constable appeared at the jail with the local militia. He intended to drag Joseph and Hyrum into court though he didn't have the authority to do so. The jailer tried to protect his prisoners, but the constable became belligerent, and the mood turned ugly.

Knowing that the jailer was risking his own life to protect him, Joseph stepped forward and shook the man's hand.

"Mr. Stigall," he said, "I thank you for your help. You are an honest, honorable man, and the Lord will bless you for your kindness."

Joseph then turned to his brother. "Hyrum? Shall we?"

Hyrum nodded and stepped boldly forward. "I'm with you, Joseph."

Joseph surveyed the crowd. There wasn't a friendly face to be seen; the hostility was so thick he could have cut it with a knife. Joseph knew the mob wanted blood, and he knew that he and Hyrum might be killed before they reached the courthouse. But, he told Hyrum, "If they take us, we shall die as gentlemen."

Just to the side of the porch, a burly soldier was glaring meanly at the prophet. In one smooth motion Joseph stepped up to the man, smiled, and locked arms with him.

"Good sir," he said. "I would be obliged if you would escort my friends and me to the courthouse."

I know a young woman named Courtney who once saw one of her friends sneak a couple of small items into her purse while they were shopping.

"*Laura!*" She whispered. "What are you *doing*?"

"It's no big deal," Laura replied.

"Yes, it *is* a big deal," Courtney insisted. "And it's wrong."

And what Courtney did next amazed me. She not only convinced Laura to return the stolen items but to tell the store manager what she'd done! I can't imagine how hard that must have been for Courtney *or* Laura. But Courtney did what she knew was right.

The man's eyes flickered in surprise. But before he could react, Hyrum locked arms with Joseph, and the two of them started down the street, dragging the bewildered soldier with them.

For a man who thought he was about to be killed, that was a remarkable way to act.

Now you might never find yourself in a situation as dire as Joseph Smith's. (I certainly hope you don't!) But when you're faced with tough choices, you can still follow the prophet's example. You can be courageous in deciding to attend your meetings. In deciding to bear your testimony. In paying your tithing. In standing up for what you know is right.

Like Joseph Smith, you can choose the right . . . even when that's hard to do.

I have a young friend named Brynn who was taking a test in the school computer lab. Two other girls were working at the computers beside her.

"I hate to use the word 'popular,' " Brynn told me. "But that's what they were. They were the kind of girls it's fun to be seen with. The kind you're always hoping will invite you to sit with them at lunch."

But after a couple of minutes, one of them leaned over.

"Have you answered number five yet?" she asked.

"Yes."

"What did you put?"

Brynn was stunned. Having Julia ask for an answer was the last thing she expected. And she couldn't believe that Julia actually wanted to cheat. She was so surprised that she couldn't even think of anything to say.

"Well?" Julia asked after another moment. "What did you put?"

At that moment, Brynn knew she was facing one of those critical decisions you sometimes hear about in Sunday School or Seminary. She was either going to offend one of the most popular girls in the school—a student she desperately wanted to be friends with—or she was going to go home feeling ashamed of herself.

> President Monson once said, "Life's journey is not traveled on a freeway devoid of obstacles, pitfalls, and snares. Rather, it is a pathway marked by forks and turnings. Decisions are constantly before us. To make them wisely, courage is needed: the courage to say, 'No,' the courage to say, 'Yes.' Decisions do determine destiny" ("The Call for Courage," *Ensign*, May 2004, 54).

Brynn paused in her story, and I was dying to know what happened next.

"I told her no," she said.

"Really?"

She nodded. "I just said, 'I can't tell you, Julia.' "

"Wow. What did she say?"

"She wasn't happy," Brynn said. "But it doesn't matter. I couldn't cheat."

Being courageous doesn't just mean being brave in the face of danger. It also means choosing the right . . . especially when that's hard to do. Consider these examples:

WEAK RESPONSE	COURAGEOUS RESPONSE
I try to live the Word of Wisdom.	I **always** live the Word of Wisdom! (And I stay away from situations where I might face temptations.)
I pay tithing when I can.	I pay my tithing first every month, no matter how much I might need the money. I trust my Heavenly Father to provide for me.
I try to attend my church meetings.	I go to all my meetings every week. And I don't just sleep on the back row! I get involved! I contribute. I answer questions. I help to make the meetings more interesting and uplifting for everyone.
I try to dress appropriately.	I've read *For the Strength of Youth*, and my clothes are always modest and appropriate.

WEAK RESPONSE	COURAGEOUS RESPONSE
I try to pray every day.	I follow the Savior's counsel to "pray always" (3 Nephi 18:15). I make time to pray first thing every morning, last thing every night, and all kinds of times in between!
I try to read the scriptures every day.	I read my scriptures every day. I ponder those things I read and search for ways to apply them to my life.
I'm trying to gain a testimony.	I've read Moroni's promise (Moroni 10:3–5). And I'm putting it to the test. I read the Book of Mormon. I ponder it. I live its teachings. And I pray about it.

Looking over the boxes above might seem intimidating. But don't get discouraged! Instead, start easy. Choose one item from the list—one you might be struggling with. Then go after that one item, doing what you can to improve yourself in that category.

Give it a try!

Ask your Father in Heaven for the strength to improve. Then, as you get better, choose another item and start working on that one too!

PASSING THE TEST

Have you ever been in an awkward situation? I have! When I became an EMT, I had to take a written test. I studied and practiced and studied some more. But the minute I opened the test, I knew there was a problem. I had been studying a practice test with several other students the day before. And the test I had now was an exact copy of the one we'd studied.

Oh, man! I thought. *What am I gonna do now*?

It wasn't just that I'd seen the test and knew all the answers. But I figured that the student who'd brought it probably shouldn't have had it. If I told my instructor, my friend would be in a lot of trouble . . . and might even fail the course.

Man, I don't need this right now, I thought. All I wanted was to take my test and do my best . . . worrying over sticky ethical dilemmas would just ruin my concentration.

I told myself that I hadn't known I was looking at the actual test the day before. But that didn't make me feel any better. I knew that if I went ahead and finished the test, I'd never feel good about it. And I knew that I wouldn't be happy with myself.

I sighed, then picked up my papers and asked my teacher if I could talk with her out in the hall. I think she expected me to confess that I hadn't studied and wasn't ready for the test. And she was shocked when I told her what had happened.

"Well," she said. "You have a bit of a problem here, don't you?"

In the end, she let me finish the test. My friend got a stiff lecture, but he hadn't been trying to cheat either. And we all ended up passing the course.

And I can't tell you how excited I was, not just for passing but for knowing that I'd passed honestly.

What's the most difficult situation you've ever been in?

↓

Are you happy with the way you handled things?

↓

If the same thing happened again, is there anything you'd do differently?

↓

Think of someone you really respect or admire. How do you suppose *they* would handle that situation?

↓

Is there anything you can learn from their example?

HE'S . . . OUT?

I know a young baseball played named Wyatt. In the middle of a tough game one day, Wyatt was on second base when the batter knocked a line drive through the gap into left field.

Wyatt took off like a rocket, rounding third and racing for home. The left fielder snatched up the ball and rifled it in. Wyatt dropped and slid, plowing over the plate in a cloud of dust.

"Safe!" the umpire shouted, waving his arms dramatically. "Safe! Safe! *Safe*!"

Both coaches exploded from their dugouts, waving their arms and shouting. One couch was yelling that Wyatt was out, the other coach shouting that he wasn't.

Wyatt was standing to the side, his uniform covered with dirt. After a moment he said, "He tagged me, coach,"

It took a second for Wyatt's words to sink in. The umpire and both coaches stopped arguing to stare at him.

"What did you say?"

"He tagged me, Coach. It was close, but he tagged me before I touched the plate. I was out."

The three men were so stunned it was a moment before any of them could react. And when one of his teammates got after him for costing the team a run, Wyatt looked the kid right in the eyes, tapped a finger against his chest, and said, "That's *not* the way I want to beat those guys . . . And It's not the way *you* want to beat 'em either."

Wyatt's team eventually won the game, but he told me that wasn't the point.

"What if that had been the winning run?" he asked. "How could I have ever been happy about winning like that?"

And then he nodded and said, "I wanted to beat those guys. I wanted to beat 'em more than anything. But it wouldn't have meant anything if we didn't beat 'em fair and square."

Now *that* took a lot of courage. And it was a good example of a young man determined to choose the right . . . no matter what.

SIX COOPED UP IN THE ATTIC

STANDING STRONG WHEN TIMES ARE TOUGH

Cameron Burns charged into the ski patrol ready room like a blitzing linebacker into a weak defense.

"Shane! Grab your pack . . . Lexi, Mike—grab your packs! We gotta go, *now*!"

I threw my backpack over my shoulders and cinched down the straps.

"What's going on?" I asked, tugging on my gloves and parking my goggles on my forehead. "Where're we going?"

"Rustler," Cameron said, naming one of the resort's most popular lifts. "They're gonna open it in twenty minutes."

Holy cow, I thought, zipping up my coat and heading for the door. *This is gonna be wild . . .*

Snow had been falling in Park City, Utah, for three straight days. Hard. There was so much snow that cars were stuck and stranded all over town. The forty-five-mile drive to Park City from my home in Orem had been a two-hour nightmare.

On the mountain itself, the wind was blowing so hard that the resort hadn't even opened the Rustler lift.

My ski patrol team had been scheduled to work the Rustler area that day, but because it wasn't open, we'd reported to patrol headquarters to wait for another assignment.

But now they were going to open the lift, and we had to be there when they did.

We skied into the storm.

The wind was howling, the snow blowing sideways over the mountain. When we reached the top of Rustler, the first thing we noticed was that our fleet of rescue toboggans was completely buried in the snow.

"You guys get those dug out!" Cameron shouted over the howl of the wind. He held a hand above his goggles and peered into the snow. "I'll start digging a path into the shack!"

Lexi and I pulled avalanche shovels from our packs and began digging out the toboggans. They were buried so deep that if it wasn't for a single handle poking up from the snow, we wouldn't have even known where they were.

I looked toward the lift as we worked. It was less than thirty yards away, but there was so much snow whipping by I couldn't even see it.

About the time we got the toboggans dug out, the resort decided not to open the lift after all. But now sixty or seventy people were stuck at the bottom of the lift. With the lift not running, we used a Snowcat to transport people out twelve at a time.

And us?

There wasn't room on the Snowcat, so a handful of snowmobiles came after us. The drivers tossed out ropes and then towed us out of the canyon like water skiers on a frozen lake.

Was it cold?

My hands didn't warm up 'til spring. (And one finger still feels kinda numb.)

Was it hard?

I went home so sore and tired I ached for a week. (I still have a bad kink in my neck.)

Was it fun?

Have you ever water skied? Can you imagine doing that in the snow, going uphill, behind a snowmobile driven by a guy who thinks he's flying a fighter jet?

What a kick!

Yeah, given the choice, I would have picked a bright, sunny day with knee-deep powder. Who wouldn't?

But it *wasn't* a sunny day. And that meant I had a choice: I could moan and groan and whine about how miserable things were.

Orrrrr, I could make the most of it, blazing into my job like a hurricane, looking for ways to make the storm more exciting, more memorable, and more adventurous.

Can you guess what I did!

And what an awesome day it turned out to be. Looking back, in fact, that cold, snowy day is now one of the most memorable of my career!

Now, I know that a little wild weather doesn't qualify as a major hardship. But it taught me an important lesson. And it reminded me that life isn't always as smooth as creamy vanilla ice cream.

We all face trials and hardships from time to time. And when they come, we have a choice. We can mope and pout and wait for things to get better.

Or (better choice here) we can put smiles on our faces and make the most of what we have.

And that's something Joseph Smith taught by example again and again and again.

In 1832, for instance, the Prophet Joseph wrote a letter that has sometimes been called his "Psalm of Joy":

> Brethren, shall we not go on in so great a cause? Go forward and not backward. Courage, brethren; and on, on to the victory!

Wow! He *does* sound full of joy, doesn't he? Like he's chock full of hope, excitement, energy, and enthusiasm. He continued, writing:

> Let your hearts rejoice, and be exceedingly glad. Let the earth break forth into singing. (D&C 128:22)

You might be thinking, *Yeah, Joseph Smith was one happy guy, wasn't he?*

But do you know where he was when he wrote that? He was in Edward Hunter's attic.

His *attic*?

Yeah . . . he'd been accused of trying to assassinate Missouri governor Lilburn Boggs. Deputy sheriffs were scouring Nauvoo, hoping to capture him, hoping to drag him back across the river to Missouri.

Joseph knew he'd never get a fair trial there, so he went into hiding. And whenever the deputies came hunting, he climbed into Brother Hunter's attic, which was so small that he couldn't stand up.

And he spent *hours* there . . . cooped up in that dark, cramped, dusty, musty attic. Away from his family. Away from his friends. Away from his home. Unable to stretch.

No, Joseph's circumstances weren't the best.

No, he wasn't having much fun.

But Joseph was able to look past his afflictions and focus on the bigger picture.

What a great example!

And right there, I think, Joseph Smith was teaching us how to endure the problems and hardships that creep up in *our* lives. Rather than sitting in the attic being miserable, focusing on the 5 percent of his life that wasn't fun, he was thinking of the 95 percent of his life that was!

Now, what about you?

When you're going through tough times, do you dwell on your problems and mistakes?

Or do you appreciate the things that are going well in your life?

I'm a junior high school teacher. One day, one of my students gave me a bad time, and I spent the rest of the day feeling bad about it. I felt discouraged, stressed out, and miserable.

> Here's more of what the prophet wrote while he was cooped up in the attic:
>
> "Let the mountains shout for joy, and all ye valleys cry aloud; and all ye seas and dry lands tell the wonders of your Eternal King! And ye rivers, and brooks, and rills, flow down with gladness. Let the woods and all the trees of the field praise the Lord; and ye solid rocks weep for joy!" (D&C 128:23).
>
> Try being that optimistic the next time you're going through a tough time!

Man!

Have you ever felt like that?

And yeah, I know I was being silly. But on the way home I was listening to a tape and heard the speaker say, "Whenever I feel discouraged, I take out what I call my 'Blessings List.' And I start reading all the things that I'm grateful for."

And just that fast my attitude changed. I began remembering all the *good* things that had happened to me that day:

- A student named Kayla brought me a plate of homemade brownies. (And she is goooood in the kitchen!)

- At lunch, a student named Braiden, who'd just transferred into my class, came up to my classroom to eat lunch with me.
- Kelly, an eighth-grader who lives around the corner, dropped by between classes "just to say hi."
- Steve, a seventh-grader who'd been struggling all year, scored 88 percent on a test . . . his best score ever!

And once—while I was at my desk hunched over a pile of papers—I looked up to see a young man named Calvin grinning at me. Calvin was the class clown . . . a boy with the personality of a firecracker and a grin the size of Texas. He had the enthusiasm of a Labrador puppy and the energy of a whirlwind.

The only problem was that this wasn't his class.

"Hey, Cal," I said, reaching out to give him a fist bump.

He bumped me back but kept pushing like it was a game of "let's see who quits first."

"What's going on?"

"Nothing," he said, still grinning, still pushing. "I'm in English, but Mrs. Davis let me out for a minute."

And so he'd come by to say hi.

How can you not appreciate a kid like that? He reminded me how lucky I was to be teaching such great kids.

> While cooped in the attic, Joseph might have been thinking thoughts like these:
>
> "Yeah, it's dirty in here. But I'll be clean again . . ."
>
> "Yeah, it's dark in here. But I'll see the sun again . . ."
>
> "No, I can't stretch or run or even stand up in here. But I'll be able to play and wrestle again . . ."
>
> "Yeah, it's lonely here. But I'll see my family and friends again . . ."
>
> No, being cooped up in that attic wasn't Joseph's idea of a good time. But he knew that being miserable wouldn't change things. And so he chose to look ahead. He chose to look at the bigger picture. And he trusted his Heavenly Father to see that everything would work out.

And you know what?

Suddenly I was feeling good again. Just that fast and I knew I didn't have any reason to feel stressed or discouraged.

I'd had an *awesome* day!

And I wasn't going to let one student ruin it for me.

Imagine having a bad day . . . one where *nothing* is going right. On the time line of success, you might feel like you're clear down on the stormy end like this:

Not so cool, huh?

But you know what? It's not where we are on the line that's important. **It's the direction we're facing that makes the difference**!

Remember that when Joseph Smith was cooped up in the attic, he was *physically* on the stormy end of the line. But he wasn't thinking of that. Instead, he was determined to be happy despite his circumstances. He was looking *forward*, facing the sun, keeping his eye on the big picture.

When times are tough, you can do the same thing!

Remember when Joseph first went into the Sacred Grove? As he knelt to pray, he was suddenly overcome by a power of such awful strength and blackness that he actually thought it would destroy him.

"I was seized upon by some power which entirely overcame me," he said, "and had such an astonishing influence over me as to bind my tongue so that I could not speak. Thick darkness gathered around me, and it seemed to me for a time as if I were doomed to sudden destruction" (Joseph Smith—History 1:15).

> While Joseph was cramped up in the attic, he did something else that impressed me. He couldn't talk to his friends, so he *wrote them a letter*! Rather than worry about those things he *couldn't* do, he worked on those things he *could*!
>
> In your life, don't focus on the things you can't do, focus on those things you can! Rather than dwell on those things missing in your life, appreciate what you have!

And how did Joseph react? In that moment of awful darkness—when he thought he was about to be overcome—what did he do?

He began to pray even harder!

That, I think, is a great lesson for all of us. And it's a great example of how to tackle the tough times and challenges that occasionally come to all of us.

> When Joseph Smith felt like he was about to be overcome in the Sacred Grove, he gathered up every last bit of strength he had and began to *pray even harder*! How can you relate that example to a problem or challenge that *you're* facing?

I was at a youth testimony meeting once when a young man said, "I know that the Prophet Joseph Smith had to endure trials, and I try to follow his example. Whenever life gets hard, I just think of what he went through and what he endured, and that gives me the strength I need to go on. I just remember that Joseph Smith could do it and that I can do it too."

I once had a fourteen-year-old boy named Travis in my geometry class. A month before school started, he was in an accident and lost his right leg. I'd never met Travis, but when I heard what happened, I figured he wouldn't be coming to school that year.

Boy, was I ever wrong!

Before the end of the first term, he came spinning into my classroom in a wheelchair.

"Hi, I'm Travis," he said, reaching up to shake my hand. "I know I'm a little behind, but I'm anxious to catch up!"

I was touched by Travis's enthusiasm. And he was true to his word. He tore into his work with the energy of a tornado, not only keeping up with the class but catching up on all the work he'd missed too.

Within a couple of months, Travis was fitted with an artificial leg, and he traded in his wheelchair for crutches. The only problem was that the new leg hurt, and he often took it off during school. It wasn't unusual to pass him in the hall and see a leg poking from the top of his backpack. And sometimes he'd pop into my classroom with a frantic look on his face.

"Mr. Barker!" he'd exclaim. "I lost my leg! Did I leave it in here?"

I loved Travis's attitude. He attacked his problems and challenges much like Joseph Smith might have.

Take a minute to work through the following checkup to see how *you're* doing. Remember, no cheating now! Don't skip ahead without answering the questions!

Ready?

Let's give it a try!

ADVERSITY CHECKUP

Circle the number that best describes you. When things go wrong and times are tough . . .

	EHHH, NOT SO MUCH				ABSOLUTELY
I look for solutions (instead of whining and feeling sorry for myself):	1	2	3	4	5
I keep on working (even when that's hard to do):	1	2	3	4	5
I follow Joseph Smith's example and pray even **harder**:	1	2	3	4	5
I count my blessings:	1	2	3	4	5
I keep a **positive** attitude ('cause I *know* the sun's gonna come out again):	1	2	3	4	5
I have faith that things will work out for me (I've got D&C 90:24 *totally* memorized):	1	2	3	4	5
I focus on all those things going **right** in my life (rather than all the pesky *little* problems):	1	2	3	4	5
I learn from my experience (lessons aren't always fun, but they *are* important):	1	2	3	4	5
I remember the Lord's counsel to "endure to the end" (D&C 14:7):	1	2	3	4	5

Finished? How'd it go?

If you circled lots of 4s and 5s, then you handle things as Joseph Smith might have. If you circled lots of 2s and 3s, you need to remember the Prophet's example and not be discouraged. (And I sure hope you didn't circle any 1s!)

The important thing to remember is that everyone goes through hard times. Everyone! But we get points just for enduring in this life. And we get points for facing our challenges with faith and good attitudes.

THE PARABLE OF THE WEEDS

President Henry B. Eyring told a story about his father. Even though he was nearly eighty and suffering from bone cancer, Brother Eyring nevertheless went to the stake welfare farm one day to help in a weeding assignment. It was too painful for him to kneel, so he laid flat on his stomach, pulling himself along with his elbows as he worked.

But did he complain?

No.

Did he moan about the pain he was in?

No.

Did he whine about having to crawl around in the dirt?

Still no!

In fact, he smiled, laughed, and talked happily with the other men as they worked, boosting their spirits as if he didn't have a care in the world.

Try putting yourself in Brother Eyring's place for a moment. Would you have been able to look past your afflictions like he did? Would you have looked beyond your own discomfort to serve your Heavenly Father?

With an attitude like Joseph Smith's, Brother Eyring did.

But that's not the end of the story. After all the weeds had been pulled, someone happened to notice the patch of ground Brother Eyring had weeded.

"Henry, good heavens! You didn't pull those weeds, did you? Those weeds were sprayed two days ago, and they were going to die anyway."

Can you imagine that? Crawling around on your stomach and elbows for hours, only to find that your spot didn't need weeding in the first place?

What would you have done right then?

Moaned about all your work being for nothing?

Whined about all the time you'd wasted?

President Eyring said, "Dad just roared. He thought that was the funniest thing. He thought it was a great joke on himself. He had worked through the day in the wrong weeds. They had been sprayed and would have died anyway.

"I [asked] him, 'Dad, how could you make a joke out of that? How could you take it so pleasantly?'

"He said something to me that I will never forget. . . . He said, 'Hal, I wasn't there for the weeds' " ("Waiting Upon the Lord," BYU Fireside, Sept. 30, 1990).

Just as Brother Eyring knew there was more to his assignment than weeds, there are often reasons for the trials we go through too. We may not know what those reasons are, but that's okay! The important thing is to keep **looking ahead**, **setting a good example**, and **finding ways to help others.**

Okay . . . time for a little straight talk. Tough problems are gonna come up from time to time. And yeah, there'll be moments when you feel discouraged. Or disappointed. Setbacks are certain to hold you back or slow you down occasionally. Friends might come and go.

Hard times are never fun, but they're part of life. And Joseph Smith's message is this: don't let the tough times destroy your happiness! When hard times come, fight through them! Work them out!

Then pick yourself up, dust yourself off—pop on a bandage or two if you need to—and get on with your life.

Like Coriantumr (in the words of President Jeffrey R. Holland), "lean upon your sword to rest a while, then rise to fight again" ("However Long and Hard the Road," *New Era*, Sept. 1983, 38; see Ether 15:24–30).

How have other great leaders handled tough times? Let's take a look:

DEALING WITH HARDSHIPS

After Lehi's family set sail in their homemade ship, Nephi's brothers tied him up and dumped him in the bottom of the ship for four days. How did Nephi react?

He praised his Father in Heaven!

While Ammon was serving King Lamoni, rascal Lamanites came and scattered the king's sheep. The other servants ran for their lives, believing the king would slay them for losing the sheep.

But Ammon? Recognizing an opportunity when he saw one, he thought, *This is the perfect time to set a good example for my brethren!*

While sailing to Rome, the apostle Paul's ship became caught in a storm. It was so bad, Luke wrote, "All hope that we should be saved was [lost]" (Acts 27:20).

And Paul? He encouraged his fellow passengers, basically saying, "Be of good cheer! Yeah, we're gonna lose the ship, but not a single one of us is going to drown!"

The Prophet Abinadi was lashed to a stake and burned. What did he do?

He bore his testimony!

Paul again: After the ship sank and everyone washed ashore, Paul was gathering firewood when a poisonous snake leaped from the wood and latched onto his hand. Everyone else freaked out, certain Paul would die.

But Paul? He simply "shook off the beast" (Acts 28:5) and went about his business.

Paul again: While preaching with Silas, he was thrown into jail. His reaction? He and Silas spent the day singing praises to the Lord. (Around midnight there was an earthquake that shook the prison so hard the doors flew open. Paul's and Silas's chains fell off, and they walked unharmed from the prison . . . my friend Ethan says *I* sing like that!)

Now, what about you?

When you start slipping toward the "stormy" end of the time line (when you're cooped up in the attic of *your* life), here are a couple things you can do:

YOUR TURN!

Back in the attic again: Even though he was the one cooped up and missing out on the fun, the Prophet Joseph wrote letters of encouragement to his friends.

Did you get that?

He was the one cooped up in the attic. But he was encouraging everyone else to stay cheerful!

When you're having a tough time, it helps to forget yourself. **Look for ways to help someone else**!

Make a "blessings list." Write down the names of people you're thankful for, activities you're excited about, things you're looking forward to. Then read it on those "stormy" days. Use it to remind you of all the things going right in your life!

When Joseph was in the attic, he could have thought, *Man, I'm gonna be so happy when I get out of here!*

That's called "futurizing." It means putting off happiness until some day in the future. In your case, it could mean thinking things like, I'll be happy when

- I turn 16.
- I can date.
- I graduate.
- I can drive.
- My brother moves out.
- I get a new teacher.
- I get into high school.
- I become a cheerleader.
- I get a job.
- I get that new outfit.
- I make the team.
- I get my own bedroom.
- I get my own car.
- I get a better job.
- I get a boyfriend.
- I get a *better* boyfriend.
- I get into AP Biology.
- I get *out* of AP Biology.

Remember that Joseph Smith didn't wait. He made the most of **where he was**, and he **appreciated the things he had**. You can do the same!

Remember the psalm: "This is the day which the Lord hath made; we will rejoice and be glad in it" (Psalm 118:24).

Yes, it might be raining.

Yes, you might have a big test.

Yes, you might be under a lot of stress.

Yes, you might have to do a service project after school.

Yes, you might have to tend your little brothers.

Yes, there might be all kinds of horrible things going on.

But **this** is the day the Lord has made. **This** is the day the Lord has given you.

Attack it with the energy you have! Make the most of it!

And smile as you do!

SEVEN

SNOWMOBILE IN THE TREES!

DEALING WITH MISTAKES

Hyrum Smith glanced toward his younger brother, who was sitting at the table, holding his head miserably in his hands.

"Joseph?"

Joseph slowly raised his head and Hyrum gestured out the window. "Here he comes."

Joseph looked. Sure enough, Martin Harris was trudging down the dusty road toward the Smith's farm. The man's head was down, his hat pulled low over his eyes.

A picture without words.

A feeling of cold dread knotted up in Joseph's stomach as he watched. He feared the worst had happened.

With Martin acting as his scribe, Joseph had begun translating the ancient gold plates a few weeks earlier. They'd completed 116 pages. Both men were excited about their progress, but Martin's wife complained that he was spending too much time away from home. Martin wanted to convince her how important his work was and asked permission to show the manuscript to her.

Joseph went to the Lord but was told no.

Martin persisted and Joseph asked again.

And for the second time he was told no.

But Martin wasn't satisfied. He pestered Joseph, begging and pleading until the prophet finally agreed to ask the Lord one more time. And this time the Lord said yes.

"*But*," Joseph warned before giving Martin the pages, "you *must* be careful with them! And you can only show them to the people the Lord specified."

Martin promised, taking the manuscript and leaving for his home in Manchester.

Joseph wasn't happy about giving in to Martin, but he didn't have time to worry about it. The next morning, his wife Emma gave birth to their first child. It should have been one of the happiest days of Joseph's life, but the baby only lived for a few hours.

Joseph was devastated. Making things worse, the difficult birth took a terrible toll on Emma. It robbed her of strength and left her on the brink of death. Worried, heartsick, and heartbroken, Joseph tenderly cared for his grieving wife for more than three weeks, slowly nursing her back to health.

I can't imagine how painful that was for Joseph. In addition to losing his newborn son, he was close to losing his precious wife too.

And in the back of his mind was the fact that he hadn't heard back from Martin Harris.

Emma knew that Joseph was worried about the sacred manuscript. And as she slowly regained her health, she told him to do something about it.

"Go to Manchester," she said. "*Talk* to Martin; get the pages back."

"But I can't *leave* you, Emma—"

"Go," she said again. "I'll be fine until you get back."

Joseph was torn. Emma was still weak; he knew that he couldn't just leave her.

But it had been more than three weeks since he'd last seen Martin Harris. And he knew he wouldn't feel peace until he had the pages safely back in his own hands again. So when Emma finally insisted, he took a stagecoach to Manchester. He was so gloomy and despondent that another traveler asked, "Are you sick?"

"No," Joseph replied. "But I've just lost my only child. And my wife is so ill that I fear she might not live until I return."

"I found that when I apologized for mistakes, things were better. . . .

"Most mistakes you can repair yourself, alone, through prayerful repentance," (Boyd K. Packer, "Washed Clean," *Ensign*, May 1997, 9).

I think anyone would have appeared sad under those circumstances. But Joseph was so grief-stricken that the other traveler knew there had to be even more to the story.

"Yes," Joseph admitted. "There is another trouble eating at my heart, but I dare not mention it."

A trouble worse than losing his son?

Worse than having a wife on the verge of death?

Wow.

It's hard to imagine the pain Joseph was suffering!

Joseph reached his parents' home in Manchester and sent a message to Martin, asking him to join the family for breakfast the next morning.

And to bring the sacred pages.

Joseph slept miserably that night, tossing and turning, fretting over the loss of his son, his sick wife, and his decision to ever let Martin take those pages.

The next morning, eight o'clock came . . . and went.

Then nine o'clock . . . ten . . . eleven . . . and twelve.

> Have you ever had to confess a mistake to your parents or some other leader . . . something that really made you feel like you'd let them down?
>
> How did that make you feel?

And then—the family's cold, uneaten breakfast still waiting on the table—Martin finally appeared, trudging mournfully down the road. When he reached the Smith's gate, he paused as if gathering his courage. Several long moments passed before he finally approached the house.

Joseph was anxious to ask about the manuscript, but his mother—insisting upon being polite—first asked Martin to eat with them. Martin picked up a knife and fork but immediately dropped them again. He covered his head with his hands and wailed, "Oh, I have lost my soul! I have lost my *soul!*"

Joseph leaped from the table, crying, "Martin, have you lost that manuscript? Have you broken your oath and brought down condemnation upon my head as well as your own?"

"Yes," Martin wailed. "It's gone . . . and I don't know where it is."

"Oh, my God!" Joseph exclaimed. "Oh, my God! All is lost!"

Joseph told Martin to return home and search again for the missing pages, but Martin said it was no use.

"I've looked *everywhere!*" he insisted. "I've torn open the beds and the pillows. . . . But it's gone, Joseph! It's just *gone!*"

Joseph wept, groaned, and paced back and forth in misery. He knew that he'd have to go before his Father in Heaven and confess that he'd lost the sacred manuscript.

His mother tried to comfort him, but Joseph was so distraught he couldn't be consoled. And it was hours before he was even able to eat.

If a person ever knew what it was like to suffer, or to agonize over a mistake, Joseph did then. On top of losing his precious newborn son, in addition to having a wife hovering on the brink of death, Joseph faced the disappointment of his Heavenly Father.

Can you imagine the pain he felt?

Can you imagine the suffering?

But Joseph did what he knew that he had to. He went before his Heavenly Father and confessed his mistake.

The Lord did censure the Prophet, saying, "Behold, how oft you have transgressed the commandments and the laws of God, and have gone on in the persuasions of men" (D&C 3:6).

The Lord commanded him to repent . . . or be stripped of his prophetic calling.

As a result of his mistake, Joseph lost the gift of translation for a while. Moroni took away the sacred plates, too, until Joseph had thoroughly repented . . . and proven that he was worthy to continue translating the ancient records.

When you make mistakes, don't beat yourself up over them. Instead, remember what Joseph Smith did. He repented. He learned from his mistake. And then he buckled down and went back to work, tackling his responsibilities even more diligently than before!

You can do the same thing!

I think there are a couple of important messages in that story. One is that everyone makes mistakes. Everyone! And if someone as gifted and inspired as Joseph Smith could make mistakes, chances are that you will too.

But when it happens, don't beat yourself up for it. Instead, remember what Joseph Smith did. He repented. He learned from his mistake. And then he buckled down and went back to work, tackling his responsibilities even more diligently than before.

And that's what you should do too. Learn from your mistakes. Repent if you need to. Then put those mistakes behind you and get on with things.

> Think about a mistake you've made. Did you learn anything from that experience? What was it?
>
> Even though the experience was painful, did it help you at all or make you want to do better?

There's another great lesson in the story of the lost pages. And that is never giving up because of a mistake. And never losing hope.

Do you remember Joseph's reaction when Martin admitted that he'd lost the pages? He said all was lost.

All is lost!

At that awful moment, Joseph probably believed that all *was* lost. He might have thought that he'd lose the gift of translation forever. That the gold plates would be taken away . . . forever. And that the Lord might never trust him again.

He might have even believed that he would lose his very soul.

But did any of that happen?

No!

> "If you have been guilty of sin or mischief, you must learn about the power of the Atonement, how it works. And with deeply sincere repentance, you can unleash that power. It can rinse out all the small things, and with deep soaking and scrubbing, it will wash away serious transgression. There is nothing from which you cannot be made clean" (Boyd K. Packer, "Counsel to Young Men," *Ensign*, May 2009, 49–52).

The Lord censured him, of course, and commanded him to repent. But after that, Joseph was able to continue the work his

Heavenly Father had planned for him . . . this time even stronger, wiser, and more committed than before.

In fact, that awful, miserable experience turned out to be a great learning experience for the young prophet.

Whenever you make a mistake and believe that all is lost, remember that the sun *will* come up again. Things *will* get better.

I know you've sung these words before, but read them again and let them really sink in:

> When dark clouds of trouble hang o'er us
> And threaten our peace to destroy,
> There is hope smiling brightly before us,
> And we know that deliv'rance is nigh.
> ("We Thank Thee, O God, For a Prophet," *Hymns*, no. 19)

Everyone makes mistakes, but that's not the point. It's what we do and how we react that makes the difference.

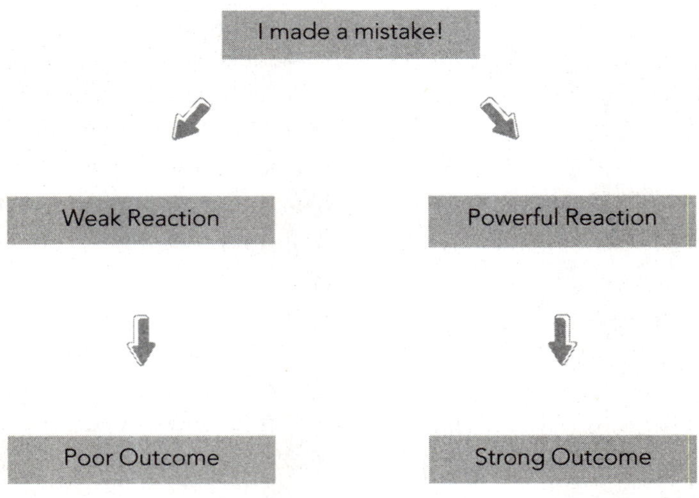

Are you still confused?

Let's look a few possible reactions to mistakes and see if things don't make a little more sense.

WHEN YOU MAKE A MISTAKE

When I make a mistake, I . . .

WEAK REACTION		POWERFUL REACTION

Beat myself up for messing up (I am such a loser sometimes).	→	Forgive myself! After all, the only people who don't make mistakes are those who don't do anything . . . and **that's** a mistake!
Keep reliving it.	→	Yeah, I messed up. But I've put it behind me. Yeah, it hurt. Yeah, it stung. But I'm a better person now for what I've learned.

WEAK REACTION		POWERFUL REACTION
Worry about it.	→	Get over it. Sure, I had a stormy yesterday, but the sun's coming up again tomorrow! (And I'm gonna **enjoy** it!)
Pretend it never happened (and hope everyone eventually forgets about it).	→	Do everything I can to make things right. If I've hurt someone, I apologize. If I've damaged something, I pay for it. I leave the situation better than I found it!
Let it ruin my day.	→	Look for something to learn. Sure I felt bad! But I've repented, I've put it behind me, and I'm moving on with my life! (I make sure this is a growing experience for me!)

See how it goes?

Just remember this: you're going to make mistakes from time to time. The important thing is to *learn from them*, *get over them*, and *get on with things*!

And here's something else to keep in mind: if you want to be forgiven, *you've got to forgive others.*

> "For if ye forgive men their trespasses, your heavenly Father will also forgive you:
>
> "But if ye forgive not men their trespasses, neither will your Father forgive your trespasses" (Matthew 6:14–15).

Can you imagine how Joseph Smith felt when the Lord forgave him for losing the sacred pages? Can you imagine the joy? The *relief*?

That might be why Joseph was always so quick to forgive those who wronged *him*.

During the course of his life, the Prophet Joseph was sometimes betrayed and wronged by his friends and family, the very people who should have been the most loyal to him. But Joseph never held grudges when people hurt him. And he always forgave those who asked his forgiveness.

In an earlier chapter I mentioned the time Joseph's younger brother William became angry with him. William began telling everyone who would listen that Joseph was a "fallen prophet."

He even managed to turn their brother Samuel against Joseph!

That had to have been hard on Joseph. But he didn't hold a grudge. In fact, he continued to pray for William and did everything he could to resolve their differences. William eventually repented and asked Joseph to forgive him. . . . Joseph did.

Another man who hurt the Prophet was William W. Phelps. After holding several key positions in the Church, Brother Phelps not only turned away but even gave false testimony against the Prophet. Because of him, Joseph spent five months in jail.

> Take a minute to think of someone who's hurt or offended you.
>
> Do you still have hard feelings toward them? What would the Prophet Joseph have done in your place?

Five *months*!

I don't know how hard it was for Brother Phelps to ask for

Joseph's forgiveness. But when he did, Joseph wrote to him, "I shall be happy once again to give you the right hand of fellowship, and rejoice over the returning prodigal."

And then (remembering that he was writing to a poet) Joseph wrote,

> Come on, dear brother, since the war is past,
> For friends at first, are friends again at last.
> (*History of the Church*, 4:162–64.)

What a great example of forgiveness! That experience might have been part of Brother Phelps' inspiration when he wrote the words, "Praise to the man who communed with Jehovah!" ("Praise to the Man," *Hymns*, 1985, no. 27.)

After Joseph lost the sacred pages, believing that all was lost, can you imagine how he felt when the Lord forgave him? You, too, might have felt that same joy and happiness after being forgiven for mistakes you've made.

And you can give that same feeling to others.

SNOWMOBILE IN THE TREES!

I was working as a ski patrolman one morning and was asked to drive a snowmobile to one of our upper patrol shacks. To get there I had to drive along the edge of a narrow ridge. To this day I'm not certain whether my ski caught an edge or if the snow just gave way beneath me. But one moment I was driving merrily along and the next I was shooting off the edge and into a ravine. (I'm not certain, but in my panic I think I pulled back on the handles, pulling the throttle and gunning the machine as I shot into space.)

The next couple of seconds were a blur, but I ended up crashing into a knot of gnarly pine trees, which kept me from plowing all the way to the bottom of the mountain. I wasn't hurt, really . . . but I wrecked a pretty expensive snowmobile.

A couple of my friends helped me get the 'bile back onto a trail. But then I had to tell my boss what I'd done.

Another patrolman told me, "The best thing to do is just march in there and tell him exactly what happened."

So that's what I did, all the time thinking, *Well, I'll never get to drive another 'bile again.*

But I was amazed at what happened. According to resort policy, I had to write a report. And I had to give a blood sample to prove that drugs or alcohol hadn't caused the accident.

But after that, my boss said, "No one will ever mention it again."

Riiiiight, I thought.

But they didn't!

On top of that, before the day was over, they sent me out on another job . . . on a snowmobile!

I couldn't believe they were giving me a second chance. But I vowed that they'd never regret it. I became the most careful, cautious driver on the mountain.

More than that, anytime anyone else made a mistake, I was the first one to overlook it. People were willing to look past my faults, and I was determined to do the same.

That was a lesson I learned from Joseph Smith. The Prophet once said that he wasn't perfect, and that if people would overlook his faults, then he would overlook theirs (*History of the Church*, 5:181).

And that's good advice for all of us!

Making mistakes is a part of life, and you're going to make them from time to time. So when it happens, don't beat yourself up over it. Instead, look at your slips and goofs as opportunities to grow. Learn from them, repent if you need to, then get on with your life! Use your experience to forge ahead stronger, better, and more valiantly than ever before!

EIGHT

PILEUP ON THE HIGHWAY!

OFFERING PRAYERS THAT CONNECT

A rain-soaked man was standing in the middle of the canyon road, frantically waving his arms. I pulled up beside him and rolled down the window.

"Are you okay?"

"There's been an accident just around the bend," the man said. "The road's slick and you've gotta drive slow or you'll slide right into it."

"Is anyone hurt?"

The man nodded. "It looks pretty bad."

"Has anyone called 911?"

"Yes. But the ambulance is several miles away. It'll be some time before it gets here."

"Okay. I'm gonna go see if I can help."

My heart was pounding as I drove ahead. I was an Emergency Medical Technician—an EMT. The bad news was that I'd received my certification just two weeks earlier. I had no experience.

None!

Yeah, I'd done okay in class . . . but I'd never, ever been on the scene of a real accident.

As I drove through the rain, I began to pray. And I mean I *really* began to pray! Lives were at stake, and I prayed with all my heart that I'd know what to do. I prayed that I'd be able to help whomever was hurt. I pleaded with my Heavenly Father for help remembering my training.

It was one of the most fervent, heartfelt prayers I've ever offered.

And I had an inkling of what Enos was doing when he cried out in "mighty prayer" (see Enos 1:4).

Has there ever been a time when you've cried to your Heavenly Father in "mighty prayer"? What prompted that?

How was that prayer different from ones you normally say?

What would your relationship with your Heavenly Father be like if you always prayed that way?

It turned out that no one was seriously injured, but that's not the point. I still remember the power of that prayer. I was desperate for my Heavenly Father's help, and I prayed with all the power and urgency I could muster. I didn't say a simple "checklist" prayer. And I didn't use trite or repetitious phrases as I sometimes did. Instead, I opened my heart and poured out my soul as I pleaded for the Lord's help.

Now, I'm sure there've been times when you've prayed that hard too. Maybe even harder.

And maybe there have been times when you've simply said "habit" prayers: the kind you say when you're tired or in a hurry and when you're just going through the motions without really thinking about what you're saying.

But when it comes to saying good, effective prayers—when it comes to saying prayers that really connect—there's a lot we can learn from the example of Joseph Smith.

The Prophet Joseph often turned to his Heavenly Father when he needed help or guidance, and he knew how to offer prayers that connected. His example can be a great guide when you need to offer a prayer that does more than bounce off the ceiling.

Let me give you a few examples.

PRAY FOR WISDOM

Take a moment and think about just a few of the dramatic events that occurred because Joseph knelt and prayed:

- He received the First Vision.

- He received a visit from the angel Moroni.
- He was baptized and received the Aaronic Priesthood.
- He received the revelation known as the Word of Wisdom.
- He received permission to show the sacred plates to men who became known as the Three Witnesses.

Remember that when the Lord used Joseph to restore his Church, he didn't give the young prophet a checklist and say, "Okay, there you go . . . have fun!"

Instead, he helped Joseph get started. And then, as questions and concerns cropped up, Joseph asked for guidance.

And the Lord provided answers.

Now, the Lord didn't send you here expecting you to muddle through life's problems without help. He's there ready to help when you need him.

And you know what else? I think he's excited when you ask!

Think about it. Don't you feel good when someone asks *you* for help or advice?

Now, you might be president of the deacons' quorum, wondering how to help an inactive member of your quorum. You might be a laurel wondering how to include the ward priests in a combined activity. Or maybe you're just wondering how to handle some problem at home, at school, or with friends. Whatever the case, I believe the Lord wants to help. And—as with Joseph Smith—he's just waiting for you to ask.

Is there a problem or question that you need help with?

↓

On a scale of 1 to 5, how sincerely have you prayed about it? (Would Enos consider yours a "mighty prayer"?)

Circle a number:

1 2 3 4 5

↓

Is there anything you can do to improve the quality of your prayers? Anything to better prepare your heart and mind for a talk with your Heavenly Father? What is it?

As I was typing this into my computer, an eighth-grade friend of mine named Hunter called me. She had been offered a chance to attend a prestigious charter school, and she didn't know whether to accept or to remain at the local junior high. Her parents left it up to her, and she was struggling to make a decision.

> President Thomas S. Monson once said, "Perhaps there has never been a time when we had greater need to pray. . . . It is through earnest and heartfelt prayer that we can receive the needed blessings and the support required to make our way in this sometimes difficult and challenging journey we call mortality" ("Three Goals to Guide You," *Ensign*, Nov. 2007, 119–21).

Now that may not sound like a dramatic problem, but to Hunter, it was important. She was so worried that she couldn't sleep. On top of everything else, school started in less than a week, so she didn't have much time to make up her mind.

"My dad gave me a blessing," she told me. "But I was still up 'til 11:30 last night praying about it."

"And what happened?"

"I began thinking about music."

"*Music?*"

"Uh huh. I began thinking about how much I enjoyed being in the school chorus . . . you know, singing and performing and going to festivals . . ."

Hunter said the charter school didn't have a music program, and just like that she knew she needed to stay in the neighborhood junior high.

"I *knew* it was the right thing to do," she said. "I suddenly felt good and calm and *happy*, and I knew I'd made the right decision."

Now, what about you? When *you* have questions, when *you* lack wisdom or insight—or when you are struggling with difficult decisions—do you "ask of God" (see James 1:5)?

When *you* lack wisdom, remember the Prophet Joseph's example.

Ask!

PREPARE YOURSELF FOR PRAYER

Joseph Smith translated the Book of Mormon in about three months . . . less time than it takes many people to read it. But that doesn't mean it was always easy.

One morning he had a disagreement with his wife, Emma, before going upstairs to work. And he was suddenly unable to translate. He struggled for some time and then went to a secluded spot in a nearby orchard to ask the Lord what was wrong.

After pouring out his soul, he went back inside and apologized to Emma. He made things right with her. And then he went back to work, once again able to translate as usual.

Joseph learned that his heart and mind had to be right to do the work of the Lord. Prayer is like that too.

> Joseph learned that his heart and mind had to be right to do the work of the Lord. Is there anything in your life that might be keeping you from connecting with the Spirit of the Lord? (What can you do about that?)

Imagine having an argument with your parents, or with your brothers or sisters, and then going off to pray for some special insight or blessing. Do you think you could hear the whisperings of the Spirit through a heart still teeming with anger?

Of course not!

If you need to communicate with your Father in Heaven, you need to be in tune with his Spirit. Your heart and mind need to be in the right place. And that sometimes takes preparation.

President Gordon B. Hinckley once said, "The trouble with most of our prayers is that we give them as if we were picking up the telephone and ordering groceries—we place our order and hang up. We need to meditate, contemplate, [and] think of what we are praying about" (*Teachings of Gordon B. Hinckley* [Salt Lake City: Bookcraft, 1997], 469).

Joseph Smith understood that. And he set a great example. Before he ever went into the woods to ask which church to join, he read from the Bible.

He mulled his question over in his mind.

He attended various church meetings and listened carefully to what was said.

He tried to work the problem out in his mind.

Only *after* doing all that did he kneel in the Sacred Grove.

Now what about you? Do you prepare yourself for prayer? Or do you simply send in your "grocery list"?

If you want to offer an effective prayer, be sure that your heart and mind are free of the clutter and impurities that sometimes collect there. Try kneeling for a few minutes before beginning your prayer. Clear your mind of the everyday thoughts and problems that might distract you. Focus on what you need to discuss with your Father in Heaven.

Then picture yourself actually talking with him. Picture him actually listening to you, because you know what? You really are talking to him, and he really is listening!

Would you like to improve the effectiveness of your prayers? Try these ideas!

1. Be sure your heart is free of impurities.

2. Clear your mind of the day's clutter.

3. Try kneeling for a few minutes before beginning your prayer. Think about what you're about to do.

4. Focus on what you need to discuss.

5. Picture yourself actually talking with your Father in Heaven.

6. Open your heart and talk to your Heavenly Father as if he's really listening . . . because you know what? He really is!

ACT!

Describing his First Vision, Joseph said, "My object in going to inquire of the Lord was to know which of all the sects was right, that I might know which to join" (Joseph Smith—History 1:18).

"Joseph's question focused not just on what he needed to know," Elder David A. Bednar explained, "but also on what was to be *done!* His prayer was not simply, 'Which church is right?' His question was,

'Which church should I join?' Joseph went to the grove to ask in faith, and he was determined to act" ("Ask in Faith," *Ensign*, May 2008, 94).

I have a friend named Kelsey who once went exploring a nearby cave with friends from her apartment complex. After crawling through the tight, dusty caverns for an hour or two, they became lost. They poked around for some time before someone made the inevitable suggestion.

"Maybe we should pray."

And so they did. The girls knelt on the cavern floor, and one of them offered a simple but heartfelt prayer for help in finding their way out.

And then the girls did the most amazing thing.

They sat down and began to chat!

Really!

After asking for the Lord's help, they didn't make a single move to help themselves.

"We talked all night," Kelsey told me. "And then about five or six in the morning, Mandy and I finally went looking for the way out again."

"And you found it, obviously."

"Oh, yeah," she said. And then she hung her head sheepishly. "It was only about fifty feet away."

I laughed at the girls' silliness, but it illustrates an important point. The Lord expects you to do your part. When Joseph went into the Sacred Grove, he wasn't just looking for wisdom. He intended to *act* upon the answer he received.

In order for your prayers to be effective, you need to follow his example. If you need help with a big test, for instance, be sure to do your part: get your books out and study!

And if you're praying for a testimony of the Book of Mormon, be sure you're following the steps outlined in Moroni 10:3–5. Be sure you're reading your scriptures every day, pondering what you read and truly, sincerely asking for a witness.

Remember the words of President James E. Faust, who said, "Blessings sought through prayer sometimes require work, effort, and diligence on our part" ("The Lifeline of Prayer," *Ensign*, May 2002, 59).

Let's try a quick discovery activity, just to focus your thoughts a little bit. It's not a test or anything—and no one's going to look at what you write—so relax and answer the questions the best you can.

Ready? Let's give it a try.

When Nephi was building his ship (something he'd never done before), he had lots of questions. And so he "did pray oft" (1 Nephi 18:3).

As you struggle with challenges, do you "pray oft"?

Remember the words of Jeremiah: "Call unto me, and I will answer thee, and shew thee great and mighty things, which thou knowest not" (Jeremiah 33:3).

Amulek said to pray "morning, midday, and evening," "when ye are in your fields," "in your houses," "in your closets, and your secret places, and in your wilderness" (Alma 34:20–26).

Speaking today, Amulek might have said to pray before you leave home in the morning, while you're at school, while you're with your friends, while you're playing ball, while you're practicing for the game, while rehearsing for the concert, or while auditioning for the play.

Do you see a pattern?

The Lord wants you to pray!

And he wants you to pray wherever you are, whenever you need him.

Amulek said to pray "over all your flocks. . . . over all your household. . . . against the power of your enemies. . . . against the devil. . . . over the crops of your fields" (Alma 34:20–25).

In modern language he might have said to pray for help with your school work, your family, your friends , your testimony, your job, your hobbies, and whatever else you need help with.

Alma echoed those thoughts, counseling us to ask "for whatsoever things ye stand in need, both spiritual and temporal" (Alma 7:23).

Did you get that?

Whatever you need! Don't be afraid to ask!

Henry W. Bigler once said, "Speaking about praying to our Father in Heaven, I once heard Joseph Smith remark, 'Be plain and simple and ask for what you want, just like you would go to a neighbor and say, I want to borrow your horse to go to [the] mill' " ("Recollections of the Prophet Joseph Smith," *Juvenile Instructor*, Mar. 1, 1892, 151–52).

Think about your own approach to prayer. Do you speak plainly? Do you ask for what you want? It takes practice! But as you **pray often**, as you **pray always**, and as you **grow closer to your Heavenly Father**, it will become easier.

Alma said to his son Helaman, "Counsel with the Lord in *all thy doings*, and he will direct thee for good" (Alma 37:37, emphasis added).

The Lord wants to be part of your life. *Every* part of your life! If you need help in school, ask! Help at work, ask! Help at home, ask! If you need help with friends, help with algebra, help with finding a job, ask, ask, **ask**!

When Lehi had his fantastic vision of the tree of life, his sons Laman and Lemuel wondered what it meant. When Nephi heard them discussing it, the first thing he asked was, "Have ye inquired of the Lord?" (1 Nephi 15:8). It's curious that Nephi didn't just sit them down and explain it all to them.

I believe he was trying to teach them an important lesson, so they could learn it all for themselves! And all they had to do was **ask**! (After all, Nephi asked, and he needed four chapters in the Book of Mormon to record the answer!)

The important thing is, Nephi's question applies to you too, whenever *you* have concerns, questions, or worries.

Have ye inquired of the Lord?

All right . . . how did that go? If you completed each of the steps, you should have several ideas for improving the quality of your prayers.

The key is to *put those ideas into action!*

Try them!

Remember that prayer is one of the most important blessings the Lord has given us. Through prayer you can receive help with many of the questions and challenges that arise in your life. Through prayer you can strengthen your testimony and become closer to your Father in Heaven.

So follow the Prophet Joseph's example. Ask your Heavenly Father for help when you need it. Prepare yourself for prayer by keeping your heart and mind pure and in tune with your Heavenly Father's Spirit.

Most of all, remember the words of the Lord, who said, "Pray always, and I will pour out my Spirit upon you, and great shall be your blessing" (D&C 19:38).

Take a moment to try the checkup below.

PRAYER CHECKUP

Circle the answer that best describes you.

	EHHH, NOT SO MUCH				ABSOLUTELY
I pray often (because it's the first, best way to become closer to my Heavenly Father):	1	2	3	4	5
I've read Alma 37:37, and I counsel with the Lord in everything I do (I know that he's interested and that he cares!):	1	2	3	4	5
I follow the Prophet Joseph's example and prepare myself for prayer (if the Prophet needs to do it, then so do I!):	1	2	3	4	5

	EHHH, NOT SO MUCH				ABSOLUTELY
I remember to thank the Lord for the help and blessings I receive (I remember Alma 7:23):	1	2	3	4	5
I wait patiently for answers (I know the Lord will answer my prayers in his own way and in his own time):	1	2	3	4	5
I have faith the Lord will hear and answer my prayers (I know he wants what's best for me):	1	2	3	4	5
I do my part to receive the blessings I'm asking for (when I do everything I can, the Lord will do those things I can't!)	1	2	3	4	5

As you look over your answers, do you see any areas where you could improve? What could you do to earn a better score there?

Is there another item you could be better at? What could you do *today* to improve your score there?

Hey, let's get to work!

When I was in seminary, my friend Ethan gave a devotional on prayer.

"You gotta wonder if Heavenly Father ever gets tired of people asking for the same thing again and again," he said.

And then (to reassure us) he gave us a list of things the Lord *doesn't* think when we ask for help. I don't remember all of them (and neither does Ethan) but here are a few highlights:

- Hey, your seminary teacher just spent a whole day on that!
- Did you even read that chapter in Alma?

- This is like the thousandth time I've had to deal with this today!
- Don't you people *ever* learn?
- Why don't you ask your bishop?

After we'd all had a good laugh, Ethan said, "No, I believe that when we kneel in prayer, Heavenly Father is thinking, 'Thank you for thinking of me. Thank you for coming to me. Now . . . let's work together and solve this problem.' "

I think Ethan had it right. When you kneel in prayer, the Lord is happy to hear from you. And he's excited to help!

NINE

THROWING FOR TOUCHDOWNS

BUILDING A TESTIMONY OF JOSEPH SMITH

Twelve-year-old Dakota Brown looked over his offensive line like an army general inspecting a crack assault team.

"Down!" he commanded, crouching behind center. "Set . . . hut! Hut!"

Dakota took the snap and dropped into the pocket, holding the football over his shoulder with both hands. He looked downfield as shoulder pads popped and cracked around him; then he lasered a pass straight down the field. Steve Hamilton caught the ball on the run and tucked it into his elbow, racing for the end zone.

"Yes!" Coach Williams shouted, dropping his clipboard and running onto the field. "Yes! *That's* the way you do that! That's *exactly* the way you do that!"

He beamed as Dakota and Steve exchanged high fives, then glanced at his watch. He shook his head and waved his hand.

"Alright," he called out. "C'mon over and take a knee."

He waited as the seventh-grade football players knelt on the grass around him, then said, "Good practice, guys. That last series was just perfect."

He grinned at Dakota. "It makes a difference when your linemen block for you, doesn't it?"

"Yes!" Dakota said, slapping one of his linemen playfully on the helmet.

"Well," Williams continued, taking another look at his watch. "I'd like to spend a little time on defense, but I know some of you have an activity, so we'll call it a night. Let's have a cheer."

He stepped back as the energized football players stood and put their hands together.

"Leopards on three," Dakota called out. "One, two, three—"

"Leopards!" the team thundered.

I stayed behind to help Coach Williams pick up gear. Our practices generally went on for another hour, but we had to cut things short that night because of a stake youth activity many of our players were involved with. I appreciated the coach being so understanding—especially since he wasn't a member of the Church—and I told him so as we walked to our cars.

"I actually know quite a bit about your church," he replied casually. "And I believe most of it."

"*Most* of it?"

"Well, I have a hard time with Joseph Smith." He gave me a look. "I mean, come on. All that talk about angels and golden plates?"

Have you ever talked with a nonmember about the Church? What was that like?

I know it wasn't the best response, but I started to laugh.

"What's so funny?" he asked.

"I'm sorry," I said, loading a bag of footballs into the back of his truck. "But it doesn't work that way. If the Church is true—and I know it is—then Joseph Smith *was* a prophet. And if he truly was a prophet of God, then the Church *has* to be true. You can't have one without the other."

The coach looked at me for a moment, then said, "Well, that sounds good and all . . . but how do you really *know*?"

There was a time when that question would have caught me off guard. But not anymore. I've always believed that Joseph Smith was a prophet. Ever since I was little, I've believed that the Church is true and that the Book of Mormon is the word of God.

But I also remember the exact moment that I *knew*.

I first read the Book of Mormon when I was a teenager. And as I neared the end, I was excited to test Moroni's promise. I prayed like I was supposed to, but (and I'm embarrassed to admit this) I'd recently had an argument with my mother. I hadn't repented as thoroughly as I should have, which meant I wasn't in tune with the Spirit.

Nothing happened when I prayed.

I'm not certain how much time passed. It wasn't the next day or the next week. It wasn't even the next month. But one day I was reading the book of Alma. Suddenly, and without warning, I felt my heart stir.

The Spirit touched me.

And at that moment I knew—and I mean I absolutely *knew*—that what I was reading was true. As much as I admired Joseph Smith, I knew that he *couldn't* have written the Book of Mormon by himself. I *knew* it was true, and I *knew* it was the word of God.

And just like that, all of the pieces came together. Because I knew the Book of Mormon was true, I *knew* that Joseph Smith was a prophet too.

And I *knew* that the Church was true.

It was an incredible experience.

Like a jigsaw puzzle, the pieces of a testimony all fit perfectly together!

Elder Glenn L. Pace had a similar experience as an eleven-year-old boy. One day he was reading a pamphlet called *Joseph Smith Tells His Own Story.*

"I was riveted," he said, "and my heart was filled with joy. After completing [the pamphlet], I caught my reflection in the . . . mirror, and much to my surprise, I was crying. I didn't understand then, but I understand now. I had felt a witness of the Spirit. My parents weren't there. My sister wasn't there. My Primary teacher wasn't there. It was just me and the Spirit of the Holy Ghost" ("Do You Know?" *Ensign*, May 2007, 78).

Isn't that a marvelous experience? You might have had one like it yourself. And if you haven't, you need to know that you can.

You don't have to be a General Authority to have a spiritual witness that the Church is true. You don't have to be a bishop or a seminary teacher. You don't even have to be president of your Sunday School

When I was serving my mission to Japan, I met a young college student named Hiro. He listened eagerly to our discussions, he began coming to church, and he read the Book of Mormon. But when we challenged him to be baptized, he wavered.

"I'm not sure," he said. "I *think* I believe it all. But I'm not sure."

We prayed together, and my companion and I bore our testimonies. And then my companion made a suggestion.

"Read the Book of Mormon again," he said. "Read it carefully. And as you finish each page, ask yourself—and I mean *really* ask yourself—is this true? Could this have come from *anyone* but God? And then pray for a witness."

Hiro agreed to try. He lived by a small lake surrounded by woods, and he began going there every morning to read and pray.

Some weeks later, my companion and I were finishing dinner when there was a knock on the door. It was Hiro, and he had tears in his eyes.

"I did as you asked," he said. "And now I know. I want to be baptized."

Hiro had an amazing experience.

The exciting thing is that you can too!

class. The scriptures are filled with stories of people like Mormon, Helaman's stripling warriors, and even Joseph Smith himself who received a spiritual witness at a young age.

"How does this spiritual witness feel?" Elder Pace asked. "It is as difficult to describe as the scent of a rose or the song of a bird."

But, he said, "Once you have felt it, you can never forget it" ("Do You Know?" *Ensign*, May 2007, 78).

Now, what about you? Do you have a testimony of the Book of Mormon?

Do you know that The Church of Jesus Christ of Latter-day Saints is true?

Do you know that Joseph Smith was a prophet of God and that he restored the Church of Jesus Christ to the earth?

If you don't, know now that you can!

"I know that you can receive a spiritual confirmation that [the Book of Mormon] is true," Elder Richard G. Scott said. "You will then know that Jesus Christ lives, that Joseph Smith was and is a prophet, and that The Church of Jesus Christ of Latter-day Saints is the Lord's Church. You will confirm that the Savior guides His Church through a living prophet" ("Realize Your Full Potential," *Ensign*, Nov. 2003, 41).

And just how do you go about doing that?

According to Elder Scott, the first step is to read the story of Joseph's first vision in the Pearl of Great Price.

"Learn of the . . . events that brought the full restoration of truth," he said. "Fix them in your mind and heart."

The next step, Elder Scott said, is to read the Book of Mormon. Even if you've read it before, start reading it today. And read it carefully.

"Try reading [it] because you want to," he counseled, "not because you have to. Discover for yourself that it is true."

And Elder Scott had this suggestion: "As you read each page ask, 'Could any man have written this book or did it come as Joseph Smith testified?' Apply the teachings you learn. They will fortify you against the evil of Satan. Follow Moroni's counsel. Sincerely ask God the Father, in the name of Jesus Christ, with real intent, if the teachings of the Book of Mormon are true (see Moroni 10:3–5). Ask with a desire to receive a confirmation personally, nothing doubting" ("Realize Your Full Potential," *Ensign*, Nov. 2003, 41).

As you follow Elder Scott's suggestions—as you follow Moroni's counsel and ask for a spiritual witness—be sure that you're praying with a sincere heart.

Don't do it because you'd *like* to know.

Don't do it because it would be *nice* to know.

Do it because you absolutely, sincerely, one hundred and ninety-nine percent *want* to know!

Finally, after you've followed Elder Scott's suggestions, be patient.

When Joseph Smith knelt in the Sacred Grove, he received an immediate answer to his prayer. As a matter of fact, he received an answer before he even finished his prayer!

But that's not the way it always is. The Lord answers prayers in his own time and in his own way. And for most people a spiritual witness does not come as dramatically or as immediately as it did for Joseph Smith.

Alma the Younger, Enos, Paul the Apostle, Joseph Smith, and many other prominent men and women have received dramatic, almost immediate answers to their prayers. But most times, a spiritual witness takes time. So don't become discouraged if yours doesn't come right away.

Be patient.

Continue to read, study, and pray.

And then wait upon the Lord.

"Be willing to endure the test of time," Elder Robert D. Hales counseled. "Do not think that it is easy to maintain a testimony" ("The Importance of Receiving a Personal Testimony," *Ensign*, Nov. 1994, 20).

If you want to know that your Heavenly Father lives—if you want to *know* that Joseph Smith was a prophet and that The Church of Jesus Christ of Latter-day Saints is true—start now. Follow Elder Scott's counsel. Remember that it worked for Joseph Smith. It worked for President David O. McKay. It worked for me and it will work for you.

Don't wait another second!

Start now!

Take a couple of minutes to work through the following discovery activity. There's no hurry, so relax and answer the questions the best you can.

BUILDING A TESTIMONY

START HERE!

Start with a sincere desire to have a testimony. "Even if ye can no more than *desire* to believe, let this desire work in you" (Alma 32:27, emphasis added).

Do you really, sincerely want to have a testimony of the gospel?

Why?

Share your desire with your Heavenly Father . . . ask him for a spiritual witness. Tell him that you're willing to do your part to receive it.

Think about the way you pray. Are you earnest and sincere as you pray? (Or do you simply say "checklist" prayers?) Is there anything you can do to make your prayers more meaningful? (Are you preparing yourself for prayer? Are your heart and hands clean?)

Begin reading the Book of Mormon. Don't simply read to finish your "page a day" or to get to the end of the chapter. Read carefully. Think about what you're reading. Mark passages that catch your interest. Apply what you learn to your everyday life.

How carefully do you read? Do you hurry through, or do you sincerely ponder what you're reading? Is there anything you can do to make your experience more meaningful? What is it?

At the end of every page ask yourself—really ask yourself—"Is this true? Is this really the word of God?"

What do you feel when you do this? What does your heart tell you?

Pray sincerely for a spiritual witness. Don't wait until you've finished the book; start now . . . pray every day. Ask the Lord to reveal the truth about what you're reading.

Are you doing this? Are you praying every day? (Or even several times a day?) What feelings do you have as you do?

Be patient. Remember that the Lord hears and answers your prayers. But he does so in his own time and in his own way. So trust him. And in the meantime, keep reading. Keep praying. Have faith that your witness will come.

You've been reading, you've been pondering, and you've been praying. What feelings have you had about the Book of Mormon?

I hope that was a meaningful experience! But before we move on, take a moment to think about how you answered the questions:

- Is there one step in the chart you could do better on? Which one?
- What's one thing you could do *right now* to improve in that area?
- Think of one more thing you could do to improve your experience.
- If you had to choose one more area you could improve in, which one would it be? (Go back and read through them again if you need to.)
- What could you do right now to improve there?

Now, take a deep breath and really think about the next question before you answer it.

Ready?

Can you think of *anything* in your life that might keep the Holy Ghost from whispering to you? Anything about your thoughts, attitudes, or actions that might interfere with your ability to feel spiritual promptings?

Is there anything you can do *today* to make things better?

If so, don't wait another second! Take care of it!

Your personal testimony of the Book of Mormon, of Joseph Smith, of the Church of Jesus Christ of Latter-day Saints, and of the fact that the Savior leads and guides his Church today through living prophets is one of the most valuable things you can ever possess.

Strengthen yours!

Start today!

> I teach a seventh-grade boy named Riley who's an avid football player. One day I saw him reading a book by Chad Lewis, a football player who played for BYU and then for the Philadelphia Eagles.
>
> "That a good book?" I asked, noticing that he was almost finished.
>
> "Oh, yeah . . . I've really liked it."
>
> "What was your favorite part?"

I was expecting him to share a story or something. But he surprised me by saying, "Let me *show* you."

And then he began flipping back through the pages. And the first thing I noticed was that it was *filled* with sticky notes. Every time he read something about working hard, or sticking it out, or anything that encouraged him to do his best, he marked it with a sticky note.

Riley wasn't just reading that book.

He was *devouring* it.

He was searching for thoughts and tips and ideas that would help him to be a better athlete . . . and a better person.

Nephi might have said Riley was "feasting" upon the book.

Now imagine attacking your **scriptures** that way. Imagine searching for thoughts, tips, and ideas to improve your life.

And imagine marking those passages so you could find them again and again.

Imagine jotting personal insights in the margins to remind you of your thoughts, ideas, and impressions.

Would those things help to build your testimony of the Book of Mormon?

Of course they would.

Give it a try! If you're not "feasting upon the word of Christ" (2 Nephi 31:20), start now!

TEN

CAMPFIRES AND TESTIMONIES

FINAL THOUGHTS

Spencer Lewis placed a handful of sticks on the dying campfire. He blew gently on the coals, and a small flame crackled to life.

"Thank you, Spencer," Brother James said. The Scoutmaster reached down and rubbed his hands over the dancing flames. "Mmmm. That feels good."

I was sitting on an old log a few feet away, enjoying the warmth of the fire. The rest of the Scouts in my troop were sitting on rocks and stumps around the campfire as we waited for our Scoutmaster to begin.

It was our fourth night at Boy Scout camp, and this was our favorite tradition. At the end of the day, after all the zany camp activities were over, we gathered around the campfire and Brother James told us stories.

The first night we were like firecrackers—full of energy and excited to be camping—and he told us tales of mountain men and grizzly bears. The next night the topic was pioneers, and then came missionary stories, which he capped by encouraging us all to begin preparing for missions of our own.

And tonight he was going to tell us about Joseph Smith.

"I don't know if you've ever thought you could make a difference in this life," he said. "But Joseph Smith was just fourteen years old—just your age—when he went to the Sacred Grove to pray. He walked in as an ordinary boy. But he walked out as a prophet."

As we listened, spellbound, Brother James told us about Joseph's first vision. He told us about Moroni and the golden plates. He told us about going on a mission and bearing testimony that Joseph Smith was a prophet of God and that through him the Lord restored his Church to the earth.

"When I was in college, I had roommates who teased me about going to church," he said. "They ridiculed me for reading the Book of Mormon and for living the Word of Wisdom."

He paused for a moment, looking at each one of us around the circle. "But I knew that Joseph Smith endured worse things than that. And whenever it became hard for me, I remembered the Prophet Joseph's courage and stood my ground."

He told us that because of his example, one of his roommates joined the Church, along with his entire family. With a smile on his face, Brother James said, "He was my best man when I married his sister in the Logan Temple."

Brother James took a moment to look at each of us and then said, "I know that the Church is true. I know that the Book of Mormon is true. Every good thing in my life—my wife, my children . . . being able to associate with each of you—is a result of belonging to the restored Church of Jesus Christ."

He paused another moment, then said, "I am so thankful that a fourteen-year-old boy had the courage to walk into a grove of trees to talk with his Heavenly Father."

I looked around the campfire as Brother James bore his testimony. The fire had died away without anyone noticing. I saw my friend Spencer wipe his eyes. Even Ethan—the most rambunctious Scout in the troop—was hanging on our Scoutmaster's every word.

I'm not sure how long we sat around the fire that night. But when we finally went to bed, I went to sleep thinking about a boy—a boy my own age—walking into the woods and coming out a prophet.

THE JOSEPH SMITH LOCK

I used to spend my summers working at Boy Scout camps. One year I ran the camp rifle range. One day Jeremy, one of my assistants, was struggling to open the lock to one of our cabinets.

"What's the matter?" a boy named Aaron asked.

"I can't remember the combination," Jeremy said, screwing up his nose like he was working out a complicated math problem in his head.

Aaron looked over Jeremy's shoulder. "Ah," he said. "The Joseph Smith lock."

"The Joseph Smith lock?"

"Yeah . . . to remember the combination, you just gotta remember Joseph Smith."

"What in the world are you talking about?"

"How old was Joseph Smith when he had his first vision?"

"Fourteen."

"Do you remember what year it was?"

Jeremy scrunched his nose up again, and I could tell he was working numbers in his head again. "Eighteen . . . twenty?"

Aaron nodded. "Eighteen twenty . . . when Joseph Smith was fourteen."

It took a second, but then Jeremy's eyes flew open. "And that's the combination! Eighteen, twenty, fourteen!"

We all laughed as Jeremy began spinning the combination like it was some sort of game. Later—as we were cleaning up before dinner—I asked Aaron how that had ever occurred to him.

"Joseph Smith's always been my hero," he said matter-of-factly. "I'm always thinking about things like that."

I was impressed. But I knew exactly what he was talking about. Joseph Smith's one of my heroes too. As a matter of fact, I have two pictures of the Prophet on my desk—and another one in my pocket—as I write this.

There have been many, many times when the Prophet Joseph's example has been a guiding light in my life.

Like my Scoutmaster, I'm thankful that Joseph Smith walked into those woods to pray.

Several years ago, I wrote a book about the three days Joseph Smith spent in Carthage Jail. I wrote it because I wanted to know what it was like to *be* there. I wanted to know what Joseph and his companions might have been thinking, and feeling, in those dark, final hours.

So I went to Nauvoo and spent time tramping through the fields. I walked down the roads, explored the temple site, and visited the restored homes.

And I hiked the dusty road to Carthage. I stood outside the jail for hours, looking up at the bedroom where the prisoners spent their final hours and trying to imagine what it might have been like to have been there.

It was an intense, riveting experience. And the question that came to me again and again was, "*Why?* . . . *Why* did Joseph Smith ever do all this?"

And the answer was, of course, because it was true. It was *all* true.

Joseph Smith knew it. He knew that God knew it. And he could not deny it.

I knew then what President Brigham Young meant when he said, "I feel like shouting, hallelujah, all the time, when I think that I ever knew Joseph Smith" (*Teachings of Presidents of the Church: Joseph Smith*, 2007, 495).

TODAY MIGHT BE THE DAY!

Do you remember the story of Joseph Smith and the stagecoach? The one I told you at the beginning of this book? Remember that the Prophet didn't know anything unusual was going to happen when he climbed into that coach. But when bad turned to worse, when people's lives were in danger, he didn't hesitate. When the Lord needed a hero, he stepped up.

You can follow his example.

No, you probably won't ever be on a runaway stagecoach. But when the Lord needs a hero to stand up for what's right, you can be that person. When the Lord needs someone to set an example of courage, you can be that person. When the Lord needs someone to be a friend to someone who's lonely, you can be that person.

And today might be the day he needs you!

Be ready!

Remember Joseph Smith!

Be that hero!

President Gordon B. Hinckley once said, "The story of Joseph's life is the story of a miracle. He was born in poverty. He was reared in adversity. He was driven from place to place, falsely accused, and illegally imprisoned. He was murdered at the age of 38. Yet in the brief space of 20 years preceding his death, he accomplished what none other has accomplished in an entire lifetime" ("Joseph Smith Jr.—Prophet of God, Mighty Servant," *Ensign*, Dec. 2005, 4).

I'm so thankful that I've been blessed to know that Joseph Smith was a prophet, that he saw God the Father and his Son Jesus Christ, and that he restored the Lord's Church to the earth. I know that he was more than a great man. And he was more than a remarkable man.

Joseph Smith was a prophet of the living God.

The Prophet Joseph once told ten-year-old Amasa Potter, "You have a great work to perform [on] this earth, and when you are in trouble, think upon me and you will be delivered" (Truman G. Madsen, *Joseph Smith the Prophet*, [Salt Lake City: Bookcraft, 1989], 55).

I want you to know that I often "think upon" Joseph Smith. And that I've been blessed as I've followed his example.

And if there's one more thing I could say to you, it's this:

Joseph Smith made a difference in this life. By following his example, you can too. I hope you'll go for it! And that you have an absolute blast as you do!

ABOUT THE AUTHOR

Shane Barker has been working with young people all his life, both as a junior high school math teacher and as the director of Boy Scout camps and high adventure bases. He has served on the faculty of National Camping School and has conducted weeklong leadership courses. An avid skier and snowboarder, Barker is an active member of the National Ski Patrol. He is a licensed pilot, a certified scuba diver, and a qualified EMT.

A popular speaker at firesides and youth conferences, Barker is the author of several books for young people. He served a mission to Japan for The Church of Jesus Christ of Latter-day Saints and later graduated from Brigham Young University. He lives in Orem, Utah.

0 26575 11176 7